the
super easy
teen
BAKING
COOKBOOK

the
super easy
teen
BAKING
COOKBOOK

60 simple step-by-step recipes

MARLYNN JAYME SCHOTLAND

PHOTOGRAPHY BY
Elysa Weitala

ROCKRIDGE
PRESS

Interior and Cover Designer: John Calmeyer
Art Producer: Hannah Dickerson
Editor: Laura Apperson
Production Editor: Sigi Nacson
Production Manager: Jose Olivera

Photography © 2021 Elysa Weitala, food styling by Victoria Woollard
Illustrations © Carrie Stephens/Creative Market, back cover; all other illustrations used under license from iStock.com

ISBN: 978-1-63807-3-307 | eBook 978-1-63807-1-839
R0

For Ethan and Cate,
with all my love—
and all the cookies.

Contents

Introduction
ix

Introduction

Hello, and welcome to the wonderful world of baking!

Whether you've been helping adults bake since you were little, or you've never baked a thing in your life, I know that you, too, can bake. This cookbook is full of super easy recipes that teens like you can make all on your own even if you don't have any prior baking experience.

When I first started baking as a teen, those initial few attempts included some big baking fails. We didn't have the internet (can you imagine?!) or any teen baking cookbooks, so I just winged it. But I kept at it—and I'm so glad I did. Baking has become one of my favorite things to do, and now my teenagers and I bake together all the time. I'm excited to share some of our family favorites with you in this cookbook.

Baking is *not* about perfection. It's a mix of chemistry and creativity, and it's meant to be fun and rewarding. It's the loving act of creating something delicious and sharing it with friends and family. I hope that, after making some of these recipes, you'll come to love baking as much as my kids and I do.

Let's get started, bakers!

Chapter 1
Kitchen Basics

Before we dive into the recipes, let's go over a few kitchen basics. This chapter has tips and tricks that can help make baking a breeze—and result in tastier treats. Feel free to flip back to this chapter anytime you have questions as you bake.

BEFORE YOU START BAKING

Here are some important things to keep in mind:

1. **Understand how the recipes work.** The recipes in this cookbook include short descriptions, serving amounts, prep and cook times, prep and dietary labels (e.g., "Really Fast" or "No Nuts"), and tools and equipment and ingredient lists to help you decide what to bake. Then, following that, you'll find detailed, step-by-step instructions that should be followed in the order each step is listed.

2. **Read through the recipes from start to finish.** This helps you get organized, which will save time, and it will help you avoid making mistakes. Before you start baking, check the cabinets and refrigerator to make sure you have all the ingredients and tools listed in the recipe, and that you understand the instructions.

3. **Set aside enough time.** Baking requires focused attention, so choose a recipe that you have the time to make without rushing. Luckily, many of the recipes in this cookbook can be done in less than an hour, and most bake in just 30 minutes.

4. **Make sure the kitchen is safe.** If your house is like mine, there may be pets, toys, and dishes that need to be cleaned up and moved out of the kitchen before you can safely start. The last thing you need is to trip over a soccer ball while baking!

5. **Set up a clean work space.** Clear enough space on a kitchen counter or table for your ingredients, tools, and work space. Gather all the equipment you need for the recipe—like bowls, measuring cups and spoons, and pans—and place them at your station so they're ready to go.

6. **Wash your hands.** Baking food safely starts with clean hands (see "Safety Tips," page 6). Get in the habit of washing your hands really well with soap and water before you start baking, and also after you touch any raw ingredients, like raw meat or eggs.

7. **Gather your ingredients.** Use the ingredient list like a checklist and check off each ingredient as you collect it. Place them in your work area in the order they are listed in the recipe. In restaurants, chefs call this *mise en place*—French for "everything in its place."

8. **Measure very carefully.** With baking, even a small difference in the amount of an ingredient can completely change a recipe. You'll need measuring spoons and cups for each recipe in this cookbook.

9. **Clean as you go.** If there's one tip my kids have heard me say over and over, it's this one. Cleaning up between steps helps keep your workstation clean, keeps your food safe, and saves you from having to clean up a big mess at the end.

Take a deep breath, jump in, and have fun!

Must-Have Baking Gear

You don't need expensive or fancy kitchen gear in order to bake impressive, delicious treats. You might already have everything you need. The following lists include all the tools and equipment you'll need to bake the recipes in this book. If you're missing any items, you can find these at low cost online, or at your local grocery store, big-box store, dollar store, or thrift shop.

TOOLS AND UTENSILS

→ Cookie scoop
→ Cutting board
→ Kitchen shears/scissors
→ Knives
→ Measuring cups and spoons
→ Mixing bowls—large, medium, and small
→ Pastry brush
→ Pastry cutter/scraper
→ Rolling pin
→ Spatulas—1 silicone, 1 offset
→ Spoons—1 large slotted, 1 wooden
→ Whisk

BAKEWARE

→ 9-by-13-inch glass baking dish
→ 8-by-8-inch and 9-by-9-inch square baking pans
→ 9-by-5-inch loaf pan
→ 9-inch round pie dish
→ 9-inch round cake pan
→ 9-inch springform pan
→ 2 (12-cup) muffin pans
→ 2 (24-cup) mini muffin pans
→ 13-by-18-inch baking sheets
→ Large mugs or ramekins
→ Cooling rack

OTHER

→ Can opener
→ Cupcake liners
→ Electric hand mixer
→ Forks, spoons, and knives
→ Instant-read food thermometer
→ Large stockpot
→ Microwave oven
→ Parchment paper
→ Toothpicks
→ Vegetable peeler
→ Wax paper
→ Zester/grater

Baking . . . in the Microwave?!

The microwave oven is like a super spy tool: On the surface, everyone knows it does one thing well (heats up leftovers), but it can do so much more!

Here are five cool ways your microwave can help you become a star baker:

1. Two words: mug cakes! Single-serving cakes microwaved in mugs or ramekins are the first desserts my daughter started baking on her own. See page 56 for one of our fave fast and easy recipes, Chocolate Lover's Double Chocolate Chip Mug Cake.

2. Use the microwave to melt chocolate or butter . . . or both (like in the Chewy Chocolate Brownie Cookies on page 38).

3. Transform the season's best fruit into delicious cobblers (like the Single-Serve Microwave Blueberry Cobbler on page 95) in just 5 minutes.

4. Warm up the yummy "glue" ingredients that hold together snack foods like granola and No-Bake Chocolate-Dipped Cereal Bars (page 30).

5. Quickly cook savory baking ingredients without messing up pots and pans, or your stove. Convenience foods like precooked, microwavable bacon make whipping up savory Cheesy Bacon Scones (page 23) fast and easy.

Safety Tips

The kitchen is usually a happy gathering spot, but it's also full of sharp objects, high heat, and potentially harmful germs. It's important to follow a few basic kitchen safety rules to avoid getting hurt or making others sick. Here are some tips to keep in mind while you bake.

KNIVES AND OTHER SHARP TOOLS

Keep yourself and others safe while using sharp tools like knives, peelers, zesters, can openers, and blenders. Here are some easy guidelines.

Use sharp knives. You're more likely to cut yourself with a dull knife, which requires more pressure and can cause your fingers to slip.

Protect your fingers when using a knife. Curl your fingers under (like claws) on the hand holding the food. This keeps your fingers safe from the blade.

Place knives on steady surfaces, where you can see them. Don't place knives on the edge of cutting boards or cover them with kitchen towels.

Don't walk holding a knife with the blade out. If you must walk while holding a knife, keep the blade pointed down by your side.

Always cut, grate, peel, and zest away from your body. In other words, move your hand downward, toward the direction of a cutting board.

Keep your hands out of blenders and food processors. Always use a spatula or spoon to scrape out food, and make sure the appliance is turned off first.

Focus on one thing at a time. When using sharp tools, slow down and give your full attention to the task at hand. Accidents are more likely to happen when we're rushing or not paying attention.

HEAT AND HOT SURFACES

The kitchen is a hot place! Follow these rules for fire and heat safety.

Tie your hair back and roll up your sleeves. This helps prevent your clothes and hair from catching on fire.

Set a timer. Carefully watch the food you're baking, as food can go from done to overcooked in seconds.

Always use dry oven mitts to pick up hot pans. Water transfers heat quickly and turns it to steam, so you could get burned if the mitts are even a little bit wet.

Keep dish towels, oven mitts, and food packaging away from the stovetop.

Watch your wrists and arms while taking items out of the oven, because the sides and inside oven door will be very hot.

Only use microwave-safe dishes in the microwave. Make sure you don't put aluminum foil or any other metals, including mugs or plates that have small metal details, into the microwave.

Never pour water over a grease fire. Water on a grease fire makes the fire spread. If it's a small stove fire, turn off the burners and place a large pot lid over the fire. For small oven fires, turn off the oven and keep the door closed; opening the door actually fuels the fire.

If there's a large fire, call the fire department immediately.

GERMS

Have you ever watched a cooking competition when the chef had to throw away a dish because it might be unsafe to eat? It's heartbreaking, but necessary. Here's how you can make sure your food is safe for snacking.

Avoid harmful bacteria contaminating your food. Use separate cutting boards and knives for meat and seafood. Never put cooked food on a dish that was holding raw meat or seafood.

Wash your hands. Wash your hands well with soapy water before you start and after you touch raw meat and eggs.

Wash fruits and vegetables. No soap needed; just rinse them well under cold water and pat them dry with a paper towel before using.

Keep your work area clean. Using soap and water or a food-safe surface cleaner, wipe down the area you've set aside to prep your ingredients. Place only the tools and food you need for the recipe in your work area.

Wipe up food spills right away. This keeps the kitchen safe for everyone.

Sneeze or cough into your elbow, away from food and from the direction of your work area.

Clean up. Clean as you go, and when you're done baking, make sure you clean all surfaces.

Pantry Essentials

When baking sweet and savory treats, you'll find yourself using some ingredients over and over again. With these pantry essentials, you can bake almost anything.

Flour: All-purpose flour is the foundation for most baked goods, including light and fluffy cookies, pies, cakes, bread, and pizza dough.

Sugar: Granulated (white) sugar, brown sugar, and powdered sugar are what make baked goods irresistibly sweet, soft, and moist.

Baking powder, baking soda, and active dry yeast/instant yeast: These are known as leaveners. Used on their own or in combination with one another, they make baked goods rise.

Salt: A little bit of table salt makes sweet food taste sweeter. It also helps strengthen dough, making baked goods stable.

Vanilla extract: This adds that classic warm bakery aroma and rich flavor to your baking. A little goes a long way!

Eggs: Large eggs are the glue of the baking world; they help bind other ingredients together.

Butter: Unsalted butter adds moisture to dough and gives baked goods that signature fluffy texture and delicious rich flavor.

Refrigerated pie crust: Use store-bought refrigerated pie crust to create fast and easy cookies, pies, pastries, and savory treats. It's the ultimate baking shortcut!

All About Butter

Butter is an important ingredient in baking. In addition to being used in recipes, butter is necessary for greasing baking pans. For the recipes in this cookbook, instead of lining a pan with parchment paper or cupcake liners, you can always lightly grease the pan with extra butter.

Baking recipes often call for butter to be at room temperature, or softened, so it can be mixed easily with other ingredients versus cold butter right out of the refrigerator. When baking recipes call for butter to be at room temperature, or softened, here are three ways to do it:

1. Set out the butter on your kitchen counter about 1 hour before you start baking.

2. Cut the butter into thin slices and set out on the counter about 20 minutes before baking.

3. Put the butter in a microwave-safe bowl and microwave for 10 seconds. Watch the butter carefully to make sure it doesn't melt.

(You can use these techniques to soften cream cheese to room temperature, too.)

About the Recipes

The recipes in this cookbook are written in a step-by-step way, to walk you through exactly what you need to do to make each dish. The ingredients are listed in the order in which you will use them. And these labels at the top of every recipe tell you more about each dish:

PREP LABELS

5 Ingredients or Less: You can bake amazing treats with 5 ingredients or less (not including water, salt, pepper, or cooking spray). Look for these recipes that have small ingredient lists but deliver big flavor.

Really Fast: Hungry *now*? Look for recipes with this label. You can prep these treats in 10 minutes or less.

No Heat Necessary: These are no-bake recipes that don't require the use of an oven, stove, or microwave.

DIETARY LABELS

No Dairy: These recipes are made without dairy products, such as cow's milk, butter, cream, and cheese.

No Gluten: Allergic to or avoiding gluten? These recipes do not have ingredients that commonly contain gluten.

No Nuts: Watch for this label if you're baking for anyone who has a nut allergy. These recipes contain no nuts.

No Soy: These recipes do not contain ingredients that commonly have soy products in them.

Vegetarian: These recipes do not contain any meat or seafood.

Always check food labels!

If you or anyone you bake for has food allergies, be sure to carefully read the ingredient labels on packaged foods. Various brands may use different ingredients or process their ingredients in different ways.

Now let's start baking!

Chapter 2
Muffins and Quick Breads

Fluffy Chocolate Chip Muffins

Makes 12 muffins
Prep time: 10 minutes / Cook time: 20 minutes
REALLY FAST NO NUTS **NO SOY** VEGETARIAN

These muffins are a favorite in my house—they usually last only a day and then they're gone! They're fluffy, light, and great for breakfast or as a snack. To keep the chocolate chips from sinking to the bottom of the muffins, toss them with a bit of flour before adding them to the batter.

TOOLS AND EQUIPMENT

Small microwave-safe bowl

Whisk

12-cup muffin pan

12 cupcake liners

2 large mixing bowls

Silicone spatula

Large spoon or cookie scoop

Toothpick

Cooling rack

....

INGREDIENTS

8 tablespoons (1 stick) unsalted butter

1 cup buttermilk

2 large eggs, at room temperature

2¼ cups all-purpose flour

1 cup granulated sugar

½ teaspoon table salt

1 tablespoon baking powder

1 teaspoon vanilla extract

1 cup semisweet chocolate chips

1. **Melt the butter.** Put the butter in a small microwave-safe bowl and melt for 45 seconds. Whisk to fully melt all the butter, then set it on the counter to cool. Take the buttermilk and eggs out of the refrigerator and set them on the counter.

2. **Preheat the oven to 400°F.** Line the muffin pan with the cupcake liners.

3. **Mix the ingredients.** In a large bowl, whisk together the flour, sugar, salt, and baking powder. In another large bowl, whisk together the melted and cooled butter, the buttermilk and eggs, and the vanilla. Slowly pour the wet ingredients into the dry ingredients and stir with a spatula until the flour mixture is fully combined. Then gently fold in the chocolate chips.

4. **Bake the muffins.** Using a spoon or large cookie scoop, scoop up the batter and divide evenly among the prepared muffin cups, filling them about three-fourths full, so the muffins have room to rise. Bake for 15 to 18 minutes, or until a toothpick inserted in the center comes out clean. Put the muffin pan on a rack and let the muffins cool for 5 to 10 minutes.

DON'T HAVE IT? If you don't have buttermilk, you can make your own by adding 1 tablespoon lemon juice or white vinegar to 1 cup milk. Let the mixture sit for 5 minutes, then stir together.

TRY THIS! Mix 1 tablespoon granulated sugar with ¼ teaspoon ground cinnamon. Then sprinkle the cinnamon sugar over the top of each muffin before baking to create an extra yummy, crunchy, sweet topping.

Sunshine Lemon Loaf

Makes 1 loaf

Prep time: 10 minutes / Cook time: 45 minutes

REALLY FAST NO NUTS NO SOY VEGETARIAN

This lemon quick bread is pure sunshine on a plate! For extra citrus flavor, add 1 or 2 teaspoons of freshly grated lemon zest to the batter before baking.

TOOLS AND EQUIPMENT

9-by-5-inch loaf pan

Parchment paper

2 large mixing bowls

Whisk

Silicone spatula

Toothpick

Cooling rack

INGREDIENTS

FOR THE LEMON LOAF

6 tablespoons vegetable oil

¾ cup granulated sugar

2 large eggs, at room temperature

3 tablespoons fresh lemon juice

1½ cups all-purpose flour

1 teaspoon baking powder

¼ teaspoon table salt

½ cup milk

FOR THE LEMON GLAZE

1½ cups powdered sugar

¼ cup fresh lemon juice

OPTIONAL GARNISH

1 lemon, zested and sliced

1. Preheat the oven to 350°F. Line the loaf pan with parchment paper.

2. Mix the wet ingredients. In a large bowl, whisk together the vegetable oil and granulated sugar until combined. Whisk in the eggs, one at a time, then the lemon juice.

3. Mix the dry ingredients. In another large bowl, whisk together the flour, baking powder, and salt. Use a spatula to slowly stir half the dry ingredients into the wet ingredients. Then stir in the milk before stirring in the remaining dry ingredients.

4. Bake the lemon loaf. Pour the batter into the prepared pan and bake for 40 to 45 minutes, or until a toothpick inserted into the center comes out clean. Let cool slightly, then take the loaf out of the pan, put it on a rack, and let cool to room temperature. Wash and dry the mixing bowls.

5. Make the lemon glaze. In a large bowl, whisk together the powdered sugar and lemon juice until combined. Once the loaf has cooled to room temperature, drizzle the glaze over the top. Garnish with lemon slices and lemon zest, if desired.

Good Morning Marmalade Muffins

Makes 12 muffins

Prep time: 10 minutes / Cook time: 20 minutes

REALLY FAST NO NUTS **NO SOY** VEGETARIAN

These zesty breakfast treats are a happy way to start the day. Bursting with bright orange flavor and topped with sweet cinnamon sugar, the muffins also make yummy afternoon snacks. Marmalade is made with citrus peels, which gives it more flavor than jam, but if you can't find marmalade, you can use jam instead.

TOOLS AND EQUIPMENT

12-cup muffin pan

12 cupcake liners

2 large mixing bowls

Whisk

Silicone spatula

Small mixing bowl

Toothpick

Cooling rack

....

INGREDIENTS

2 large eggs

¾ cup orange marmalade

¼ cup milk

6 tablespoons vegetable oil

½ teaspoon vanilla extract

2 cups all-purpose flour

2 teaspoons baking powder

½ teaspoon table salt

4 tablespoons granulated sugar, divided

½ teaspoon ground cinnamon

1. Preheat the oven to **425°F**. Line the muffin pan with the cupcake liners.

2. **Beat the eggs and mix the wet ingredients.** In a large bowl, beat the eggs with a whisk. Then whisk in the marmalade, milk, oil, and vanilla, one at a time, waiting until each is well incorporated before adding the next.

3. **Mix the dry ingredients.** In another large bowl, whisk together the flour, baking powder, salt, and 2 tablespoons of sugar.

4. **Combine the dry and wet ingredients.** Slowly pour the dry ingredients into the bowl with the wet ingredients and use a spatula to gently fold the dry ingredients into the wet, until everything is fully combined and no dry ingredients can be seen.

5. **Make the topping.** In a small bowl, whisk together the remaining 2 tablespoons of sugar and the cinnamon.

6. **Bake the muffins.** Slowly pour or spoon the batter into the prepared muffin pan, filling each cup about three-fourths full. Sprinkle the tops with the cinnamon sugar and bake for 5 minutes. Then, while keeping the oven door closed, lower the heat to 375°F and continue baking for another 15 minutes, or until a toothpick inserted into the middle of a muffin comes out clean. Put the pan on a rack and let cool for 10 minutes.

SWITCH IT UP! Switch up the flavor by replacing the orange marmalade with lemon, lime, or grapefruit marmalade or jam. You can also switch out the vanilla extract and instead use orange, lemon, or lime extract for super-citrusy muffins.

TRY THIS! Want even *more* orange flavor? Try adding ¼ cup orange juice to the batter. You can also add 1 teaspoon grated orange zest to the cinnamon-sugar topping.

Classic Banana Bread

Makes 1 loaf

Prep time: 15 minutes / Cook time: 45 minutes

NO NUTS **NO SOY** VEGETARIAN

Got a couple of bananas that are turning brown? Overripe bananas become superstar baking ingredients in the magic that is banana bread. This is a version of our family recipe that my kids have loved since they were little. We hope you'll go bananas for it, too!

TOOLS AND EQUIPMENT

9-by-5-inch loaf pan

Parchment paper

2 large mixing bowls

Fork

Whisk

Silicone spatula

Toothpick

Cooling rack

INGREDIENTS

2 large ripe bananas

6 tablespoons vegetable oil

1 cup packed light brown sugar

2 large eggs

½ cup milk

2 cups all-purpose flour

1 tablespoon baking powder

½ teaspoon baking soda

¼ teaspoon table salt

½ teaspoon ground cinnamon

1. Preheat the oven to 350°F. Line the loaf pan with parchment paper.

2. Mash the bananas. Peel the bananas. In a large bowl, mash the bananas well with a fork. Whisk in the vegetable oil until combined. Then, one at a time, whisk in the brown sugar, eggs, and milk.

3. Mix the dry ingredients. In another large bowl, whisk together the flour, baking powder, baking soda, salt, and cinnamon.

4. Combine the wet and dry ingredients. Using a spatula, mix the dry ingredients gradually into the wet ingredients, folding the mixtures together until you can no longer see any dry flour.

5. Bake the bread. Pour the batter into the prepared pan and bake for 45 minutes, or until a toothpick inserted into the center of the bread comes out clean. Place the pan on a rack and let cool for 5 to 10 minutes.

Gingerbread Spice Muffins

Makes 12 muffins
Prep time: 10 minutes / Cook time: 25 minutes
REALLY FAST NO NUTS NO SOY VEGETARIAN

Although these muffins are full of yummy winter holiday spices, we love baking them year-round. They make the house smell amazing while they are baking. Top these with store-bought cream cheese frosting or the frosting used in the Microwave Mini Carrot Cakes (page 66) for another layer of flavor.

TOOLS AND EQUIPMENT

Small microwave-safe bowl

Whisk

12-cup muffin pan

12 cupcake liners

2 large mixing bowls

Silicone spatula

Tablespoon

Toothpick

Cooling rack

INGREDIENTS

8 tablespoons (1 stick) unsalted butter

2¼ cups all-purpose flour

1½ teaspoons baking soda

1 tablespoon ground ginger

1½ teaspoons ground cinnamon

½ teaspoon ground cloves

½ teaspoon table salt

½ cup packed light brown sugar

¾ cup molasses

2 large eggs

1 cup buttermilk

1 teaspoon vanilla extract

1. **Preheat the oven to 400°F.** Put the butter in a small microwave-safe bowl and melt for 45 seconds. Whisk to fully melt all the butter. Set it on the counter to cool. Line the muffin pan with the cupcake liners.

2. **Mix the ingredients.** In a large bowl, whisk together the flour, baking soda, ginger, cinnamon, cloves, and salt. In another large bowl, whisk together the melted butter, the brown sugar, and molasses, then beat in the eggs, buttermilk, and vanilla. Slowly add the wet ingredients to the dry ingredients, mixing until well combined.

3. **Bake the muffins.** Spoon the batter into the prepared muffin cups until about three-fourths full. Bake for 5 minutes, then turn down the heat to 375°F and continue baking for 15 to 18 more minutes, or until a toothpick inserted into the center comes out clean. Place the pan on a rack to cool for 5 to 10 minutes.

Cheesy Bacon Scones

Makes 8 scones

Prep time: 15 minutes / Cook time: 30 minutes

NO NUTS NO SOY

These scones are buttery, cheesy, and full of bacon. To save time, you could also use precooked bacon that you can just reheat in the microwave.

TOOLS AND EQUIPMENT

Baking sheet

Parchment paper

Paper towel

Medium microwave-safe plate

Cutting board

Knife or kitchen shears

Plate

Large mixing bowl

Whisk

Silicone spatula

Pastry cutter or knife

Pastry brush

INGREDIENTS

6 slices bacon

4 tablespoons (½ stick) unsalted butter, cold

1 small bunch fresh chives

2 cups all-purpose flour, plus more for rolling out the dough

½ teaspoon table salt

1 tablespoon baking powder

2 teaspoons granulated sugar

1 cup shredded mild or sharp cheddar cheese

1 cup plus 2 tablespoons heavy cream, divided

1. **Preheat the oven to 425°F.** Line the baking sheet with parchment paper.

2. **Cook the bacon.** Place a paper towel on a medium microwave-safe plate. Place the bacon slices on the towel and microwave for 5 to 6 minutes, or until the bacon is cooked to your preferred crispness. Once the bacon is cool, crumble it into small pieces.

3. **Cut up the butter and chives.** Cut the butter into several small cubes on a cutting board. Then, either chop the chives with a knife or snip off small pieces with kitchen shears; you will need about ⅓ cup. Remove the butter and chives to a plate and wipe down the cutting board.

4. **Mix the ingredients.** In a large bowl, whisk together the flour, salt, baking powder, and sugar. Add the butter cubes and, using your hands, press the

Continued on next page

butter with your fingers into the flour. Mix with your hands until the dough is crumbly; it's okay if some of the butter is still in small cubes. Then add the cheese, chives, and bacon and use a spatula to fold them until combined. Pour in 1 cup of cream and stir to form a crumbly dough.

5. Form the scones. Sprinkle the cutting board with some flour. Put the dough on the cutting board and shape it into a smooth 7-inch round disk about 1 inch thick. Use a pastry cutter or knife to cut the dough into 8 pie wedges. The dough might still be a bit crumbly in some spots. Use your fingers to press the tops and sides of each scone to help keep its shape. Place the scones on the prepared baking sheet, leaving at least 2 inches of space between them, as the dough will spread during baking.

6. Brush the scones. Using a pastry brush, brush the remaining 2 tablespoons of cream onto the tops of the scones. This gives them a nice golden finish when they're done baking.

7. Bake the scones. Place the baking sheet in the oven and bake the scones for 25 to 30 minutes. When the tops and sides are slightly golden brown, remove them from the oven, and let them cool for a few minutes on the baking sheet.

TRY THIS! Craving something sweet? You can substitute your favorite fruit for the bacon, cheese, and chives, and add an extra 2 teaspoons sugar to the batter. Then, sprinkle coarse sanding sugar, sugar in the raw, or cinnamon sugar on the tops just before baking.

Pull-Apart Sticky Cinnamon Sugar Bread

Makes 8 servings

Prep time: 10 minutes / Cook time: 30 minutes

5 INGREDIENTS OR LESS REALLY FAST **NO NUTS** **NO SOY** VEGETARIAN

This bread, also known as monkey bread (a funny name for a seriously irresistible treat), is traditionally made in a Bundt cake pan, but I find it bakes more evenly—and each piece has more buttery goodness—when made in a flat baking dish.

TOOLS AND EQUIPMENT

9-by-13-inch glass baking dish

Knife

Large mixing bowl

Small mixing bowl

Medium microwave-safe bowl

Whisk

Instant-read thermometer

Cooling rack

INGREDIENTS

Nonstick cooking spray (optional)

8 tablespoons (1 stick) unsalted butter, plus more for greasing (optional)

2 (16.3-ounce) tubes refrigerated biscuit dough (not flaky)

1 cup granulated sugar

3 teaspoons ground cinnamon

½ cup packed dark or light brown sugar

1. Preheat the oven to 375°F. Spray the baking dish with nonstick cooking spray or lightly grease with extra butter.

2. Slice the biscuits. Open the tubes of dough, unroll, and slice each biscuit into 4 to 6 pieces. Separate the pieces and place them in a large bowl.

3. Mix the ingredients. In a small bowl, whisk together the granulated sugar and cinnamon. Sprinkle the cinnamon sugar over the biscuit pieces and toss with your hands to coat. Spread out the biscuit pieces evenly in the prepared baking dish.

4. Microwave the butter. Put the butter in a medium microwave-safe bowl and melt for 45 seconds. Whisk to fully melt all the butter. Whisk the brown sugar into the melted butter and pour evenly over the biscuit pieces.

5. Bake the bread. Place the baking dish in the oven and bake for 30 minutes, or until the middle is fully cooked (an instant-read thermometer will read 190°F). Place the baking dish on a rack and let cool for 5 to 10 minutes.

Chapter 3
Cookies, Bars, and Bites

Ultimate Classic Chocolate Chip Cookies

Makes 48 cookies
Prep time: 10 minutes, plus 20 minutes to chill / Cook time: 15 minutes
NO NUTS NO SOY VEGETARIAN

Every baker needs a good go-to chocolate chip cookie recipe. This one is a classic that my kids and I have been baking for years. If you want extra chewy cookies, try refrigerating the dough for longer than the recipe calls for. Refrigerating the dough for about an hour creates an even softer cookie center.

TOOLS AND EQUIPMENT

2 large mixing bowls

Whisk

Hand mixer

Silicone spatula

2 baking sheets

Parchment paper

Tablespoon

Cooling rack

INGREDIENTS

2½ cups all-purpose flour

1 teaspoon baking soda

½ teaspoon table salt

1 cup (2 sticks) unsalted butter, at room temperature (see page 9)

1 cup packed light brown sugar

½ cup granulated sugar

2 large eggs

2 teaspoons vanilla extract

2 cups semisweet chocolate chips

1. **Mix the ingredients.** In a large bowl, whisk together the flour, baking soda, and salt. In another large bowl, use a hand mixer on high speed to beat the butter, brown sugar, and granulated sugar for 2 to 3 minutes, just until the mixture turns light, smooth, and creamy. Add the eggs and vanilla and mix on low until evenly combined, scraping down the bowl with a spatula as needed. Add the flour mixture to the egg mixture and beat the ingredients together on low speed just until you no longer see any white spots of flour. It's important not to overmix the batter. Use the spatula to gently mix the chocolate chips into the batter.

2. **Chill the batter.** Refrigerate the batter in the bowl for 20 minutes.

3. **Preheat the oven.** While the batter chills, preheat the oven to 350°F. Line 2 baking sheets with parchment paper.

4. **Bake the cookies.** Use a tablespoon to scoop out the cookie dough by heaping spoonfuls and use your hands to roll the dough into about 48 small balls, until the dough is used up. Place the dough balls on the prepared baking sheets, leaving about 2 inches of space between the balls, as the dough will spread during baking. Bake for 10 to 13 minutes, just until the edges start to turn golden brown. Allow the cookies to cool for 5 minutes on the sheet, then move them to a rack to cool completely.

OOPS . . . Did you forget to take the butter out of the fridge to soften to room temperature at least 30 minutes before you started baking? You can microwave the butter for 7 to 10 seconds to help soften it. Be sure not to melt it, because melted or hot butter will cause your cookies to spread thin when they bake.

TRY THIS! Add a handful of chopped pecans or walnuts to the batter for some yummy crunch.

No-Bake Chocolate-Dipped Cereal Bars

Makes 12 bars

Prep time: 5 minutes, plus 10 minutes to chill / Cook time: 5 minutes

5 INGREDIENTS OR LESS NO SOY VEGETARIAN

Whip up these crunchy, sweet cereal bars in minutes! Best enjoyed the day of, these make great team sports snacks or after-school treats with friends. If you live in a humid climate or you make these during warm weather, store them in the refrigerator until you're ready to eat them.

TOOLS AND EQUIPMENT

8-by-8-inch square baking pan

Parchment paper

Large microwave-safe bowl

Whisk

Silicone spatula

Cutting board

Pastry cutter

INGREDIENTS

6 tablespoons (¾ stick) unsalted butter

½ cup honey

¼ cup peanut butter

4 cups Cheerios cereal

8 ounces baking chocolate or 1½ cups chocolate melting wafers

1. Line the baking pan with parchment paper.

2. Make the bars. In a large microwave-safe bowl, melt the butter, honey, and peanut butter. Whisk together and then use a spatula to mix the cereal into the bowl. Mix until the cereal is evenly coated. Pour the mixture into the prepared pan and press down into an even layer. Wash and dry the microwave-safe bowl.

3. Melt the chocolate. Break the chocolate into smaller pieces and put in the microwave-safe bowl. Microwave for 30 seconds. Whisk, then microwave again for 30 more seconds, until the chocolate is melted. Whisk until smooth. Pour the chocolate over the cereal mixture, using the spatula to spread the chocolate evenly across the top. Chill the bars in the refrigerator for 10 minutes.

4. Slice the bars. Once the chocolate has cooled, flip over the pan onto a cutting board. Use a pastry cutter to slice into rectangular bars.

Three-Ingredient Peanut Butter Cookies

Makes 30 cookies

Prep time: 5 minutes / Cook time: 10 minutes

5 INGREDIENTS OR LESS REALLY FAST NO DAIRY **NO GLUTEN NO SOY** VEGETARIAN

Peanut butter cookies are classic, and they don't get much easier than this. With just three ingredients that you probably already have in the house, these cookies will satisfy your cookie craving.

TOOLS AND EQUIPMENT

2 baking sheets

Parchment paper

Large mixing bowl

Hand mixer or silicone spatula

Teaspoon

Fork

Cooling rack

INGREDIENTS

1 cup creamy peanut butter

1 cup granulated sugar

1 large egg

1. **Preheat the oven to 350°F.** Line 2 baking sheets with parchment paper.

2. **Mix the ingredients.** In a large bowl, use a hand mixer on medium speed or a silicone spatula to mix the peanut butter, sugar, and egg just until the mixture is smooth and creamy.

3. **Form the cookies.** Use a teaspoon to scoop out heaping teaspoonfuls of dough until you have about 30 cookies. Using your hands, roll the mixture into small balls. Place the balls on the prepared baking sheets. Leave about 2 inches of space between the balls, as the dough will spread during baking. Flatten each ball with a fork to create the classic crisscross peanut butter cookie pattern.

4. **Bake the cookies.** Place the baking sheets in the oven and bake for 10 minutes. Cool the cookies on the baking sheets for 2 minutes, then move them to a rack to cool for a few more minutes.

TRY THIS! Bump up the sweetness level by rolling the unbaked dough balls in a bowl of sanding sugar (decorating sugar that is thicker than regular granulated sugar), then bake according to the recipe.

Irresistible Edible Cookie Dough Bites

Makes 24 dough bites
Prep time: 10 minutes

REALLY FAST **NO HEAT NECESSARY NO SOY** VEGETARIAN

Nobody can resist cookie dough, especially in cute, fun little snack-size bites! These are safe to eat because we use coconut flour instead of egg and all-purpose flour, both of which can be unsafe to eat raw.

TOOLS AND EQUIPMENT

Large mixing bowl

Hand mixer

Silicone spatula

Teaspoon

INGREDIENTS

8 tablespoons (1 stick) unsalted butter, at room temperature (see page 9)

½ cup packed light brown sugar

2 tablespoons granulated sugar

1 tablespoon milk

1 teaspoon vanilla extract

1 cup coconut flour

½ cup semisweet mini chocolate chips

1. **Mix the ingredients.** In a large bowl, use a hand mixer on high speed to cream the butter with the brown and granulated sugars until light and fluffy, about 2 minutes. Pour in the milk and vanilla and mix until just combined. Slowly mix in the flour. Using a spatula, fold in the chocolate chips.

2. **Shape the bites.** The dough will be a little crumbly, which is okay. Use your hands to press heaping teaspoonfuls of dough together to form 24 small dough balls.

DON'T HAVE IT? If you don't have coconut flour, you can make all-purpose flour safe to eat by baking it on a rimmed baking sheet at 350°F for 5 minutes, then cooling it completely.

TRY THIS! Instead of chocolate chips, use mini M&M candies, butterscotch chips, or white chocolate chips. You can also substitute almond extract for the vanilla.

Chocolate Glazed Donut Holes

Makes 3 dozen donut holes
Prep time: 10 minutes / Cook time: 15 minutes
REALLY FAST NO NUTS NO SOY VEGETARIAN

These fun little bites are baked in a mini muffin pan and are shaped almost like mini muffins but have the texture and taste of glazed old-fashioned chocolate cake donuts. The secret shortcut ingredient? Cake mix!

TOOLS AND EQUIPMENT

2 (24-cup) mini muffin pans

Large mixing bowl

Whisk

Toothpick

Tablespoon

Cooling rack

....

INGREDIENTS

Nonstick cooking spray

1 (15.25-ounce) box devil's food chocolate cake mix

1 large egg

¼ cup vegetable oil

1 cup water

2 cups powdered sugar

¼ cup milk

1 teaspoon vanilla extract

1. **Preheat the oven to 350°F.** Spray 2 mini muffin pans with nonstick cooking spray.

2. **Mix the ingredients.** In a large bowl, whisk together the cake mix, egg, oil, and water. Spoon the mixture into the prepared muffin pans, filling 36 of the cups just a little more than halfway.

3. **Bake the donut holes.** Place the pans in the oven and bake for 9 to 12 minutes, until a toothpick inserted into the middle of a donut hole comes out clean. Allow the donut holes to cool in the pans for 5 minutes, then transfer them to a rack to cool.

4. **Make the glaze.** While the donut holes cool, wash and dry the large bowl. Combine the powdered sugar, milk, and vanilla in the bowl. Once the donut holes have cooled completely, spoon the glaze over the tops. Let the glaze set, about 5 minutes.

SWITCH IT UP! Use the same donut ingredients to make 12 full-size Devil's Food Cupcakes in a regular muffin pan! Instead of the glaze, make frosting by beating together 8 tablespoons (1 stick) room-temperature unsalted butter, 1 softened (8-ounce) package cream cheese, 4 cups powdered sugar, and 2 teaspoons vanilla extract. (See page 9 for bringing butter to room temperature and softening cream cheese.)

Melt-in-Your-Mouth Lemon Bars

Makes 12 lemon bars
Prep time: 15 minutes, plus 30 minutes to chill / Cook time: 25 minutes
NO NUTS **NO SOY** VEGETARIAN

With a thick, sugary shortbread crust and bright, citrusy lemon-curd topping, these lemon bars put a smile on everyone's face. To really kick them out of the park, add a layer of whipped topping or a dollop of whipped cream on top of each square before serving.

TOOLS AND EQUIPMENT

9-by-9-inch square baking pan

Parchment paper

2 large mixing bowls

Hand mixer

Whisk

Cooling rack

....

INGREDIENTS

FOR THE CRUST

14 tablespoons (1¾ sticks) unsalted butter, at room temperature (see page 9)

½ cup granulated sugar

½ teaspoon vanilla extract

2 cups all-purpose flour

½ teaspoon kosher salt

FOR THE FILLING

¼ cup all-purpose flour

1 cup granulated sugar

3 large eggs

½ cup fresh lemon juice (from about 2 lemons)

1. **Preheat the oven to 350°F.** Line the baking pan with parchment paper.

2. **Make the crust.** In a large bowl, use a hand mixer on medium speed to beat the butter and sugar together until combined. Beat in the vanilla. In another large bowl, whisk together the flour and salt. Slowly add it to the butter mixture and beat until the dough starts to form a ball.

3. **Prepare the crust.** Press the dough into the prepared baking pan, using your hands to gently even out the dough across the bottom and up the sides. Make sure there are no cracks in the dough or along the sides where the filling would be able to seep through.

4. **Make the filling.** In the large bowl that held the flour, whisk together the flour and sugar. Then whisk in the eggs, one at a time, until fully incorporated. Whisk in the lemon juice.

5. **Bake the bars.** Pour the filling over the crust and bake the bars for 20 to 25 minutes, until the center is no longer jiggly. Put the pan on a rack and allow the bars to cool at room temperature until the pan is no longer hot. Then chill the bars in the refrigerator for at least 30 minutes, until set. Cut into bars and serve.

OOPS . . . Did your crust rise to the top while baking, with the lemon filling ending up on the bottom? That happens when there are cracks in the crust and the filling finds a way down through the crust. It still tastes delicious, and you can simply flip the pan over a large plate to get the lemon curd on top. To avoid this happening in the future, make sure your crust is tightly packed into the bottom of the pan, with no cracks.

Cute Confetti Cookies with Rainbow Sprinkles

Makes about 27 cookies

Prep time: 20 minutes / Cook time: 10 minutes

NO NUTS **NO SOY** VEGETARIAN

Everything's better with sprinkles! Easy butter cookies are extra fun, thanks to rainbow sprinkles. Slicing the butter helps it soften faster, and using your hands for a final mix allows you to form the dough and combine the ingredients evenly.

TOOLS AND EQUIPMENT

2 baking sheets

Parchment paper

Large mixing bowl

Silicone spatula

Shallow bowl

Small drinking glass

INGREDIENTS

½ cup granulated sugar

1 large egg

8 tablespoons (1 stick) unsalted butter, at room temperature (see page 9)

1½ cups all-purpose flour

½ teaspoon baking soda

½ teaspoon vanilla extract

½ cup rainbow sprinkles

1. **Preheat the oven to 400°F.** Line 2 baking sheets with parchment paper.

2. **Mix the ingredients.** In a large bowl, use a spatula to mix the sugar, egg, and butter. Then mix in the flour, baking soda, and vanilla. Using your hands, mix all the ingredients together to form the dough.

3. **Shape and decorate the cookies.** Place the sprinkles in a shallow bowl. Shape the dough into 1-inch balls (you'll get about 27), then roll each ball in the sprinkles. Place the dough balls on the prepared baking sheets. Leave about 2 inches of space between the balls, as the dough will spread during baking. Then use the bottom of a glass to gently flatten the top of each ball.

4. **Bake the cookies.** Place the baking sheets in the oven and bake for 6 to 8 minutes, until the edges are lightly browned. Remove from the oven and let cool completely on the baking sheets.

Red Velvet Crinkle Cookies

Makes about 20 cookies
Prep time: 15 minutes / Cook time: 10 minutes
5 INGREDIENTS OR LESS NO NUTS NO SOY VEGETARIAN

The festive red color makes these cookies great for Valentine's Day or Christmas, but they're delicious year-round, so don't keep them for special occasions! Boxed cake mix gives them the soft and fluffy texture of classic crinkle cookies.

TOOLS AND EQUIPMENT

Baking sheet

Parchment paper

Large microwave-safe bowl

Whisk

Shallow medium bowl

Wooden spoon

Cooling rack

INGREDIENTS

8 tablespoons (1 stick) unsalted butter

½ cup powdered sugar

1 (15.25-ounce) box red velvet cake mix

2 large eggs

1 tablespoon grated lemon zest

1. **Preheat the oven to 375°F.** Line the baking sheet with parchment paper.

2. **Prep the ingredients.** In a large microwave-safe bowl, melt the butter for 45 seconds. Whisk until all the butter is melted. Set it on the counter to cool. Place the powdered sugar in a shallow medium bowl.

3. **Mix the ingredients.** Once the butter has cooled for a minute or so, use a wooden spoon to mix in the cake mix, eggs, and lemon zest until just blended.

4. **Shape the cookies.** Using your hands, shape the dough into 1½- to 2-inch balls (you'll get about 20). Roll the balls in the sugar until completely coated. Place the balls on the prepared baking sheet. Leave about 2 inches of space between the balls, as the dough will spread during baking.

5. **Bake the cookies.** Place the baking sheet in the oven and bake for 8 to 10 minutes, until the cookies appear set on the outside and puffed in the center. Allow the cookies to cool on the baking sheet for a minute or so before transferring them to a rack to cool completely.

TRY THIS! You can use this same recipe with almost any flavor of cake mix. Try chocolate, vanilla, or strawberry crinkle cookies!

Chewy Chocolate Brownie Cookies

Makes about 20 cookies
Prep time: 15 minutes / Cook time: 15 minutes
NO NUTS **NO SOY** VEGETARIAN

These cookies are a family favorite. They're chewy and soft, with the fluffiness of brownies. As they cool down, the tops form a slight crinkle-cookie effect. For added flourish, sprinkle a few pieces of flaky sea salt on the top of the cookies after they come out of the oven.

TOOLS AND EQUIPMENT

2 baking sheets

Parchment paper

Medium microwave-safe bowl

Whisk

2 large mixing bowls

Hand mixer

Tablespoon

....

INGREDIENTS

8 ounces dark baking chocolate

11 tablespoons unsalted butter

2 large eggs

¾ cup granulated sugar

½ cup light brown sugar

1¼ cups cake flour

3 tablespoons unsweetened cocoa powder

1 teaspoon baking powder

¼ teaspoon table salt

1. **Preheat the oven to 350°F.** Line 2 baking sheets with parchment paper.

2. **Melt the chocolate mixture.** Break the chocolate into small pieces and put in a medium microwave-safe bowl along with the butter. Melt, pulsing for 45 seconds at a time, until the chocolate and butter are fully melted, whisking between pulses.

3. **Mix the wet ingredients.** In a large bowl, use a hand mixer on high speed to beat together the eggs, granulated sugar, and brown sugar for 5 full minutes. The mixture will be light and fluffy. Pour the melted chocolate mixture into the bowl with the eggs and sugar, then beat together for 1 minute.

4. **Mix the dry ingredients and blend.** In another large bowl, whisk together the cake flour, cocoa powder, baking powder, and salt until well blended. Slowly add the dry mixture to the wet mixture and mix just until all ingredients are blended.

5. **Scoop the dough.** Using a tablespoon, scoop out the dough (it will be wet and gooey) to form about 20 cookies on the prepared baking sheets. Leave about 2 inches of space between the cookies, as the dough will spread during baking.

6. **Bake the cookies.** Place the baking sheets in the oven and bake for 10 to 12 minutes. The center of the cookies will be soft and fudgy and slightly shiny. Allow the cookies to sit on the baking sheets for 15 to 20 minutes before eating.

DON'T HAVE IT? If you don't have cake flour, sift together 1 cup plus 2 tablespoons all-purpose flour and 2 tablespoons cornstarch into a bowl and use that instead of the cake flour.

No-Bake Cookies and Cream Truffles

Makes about 30 truffles
Prep time: 15 minutes, plus 20 minutes to chill

5 INGREDIENTS OR LESS   NO NUTS   **NO SOY**   VEGETARIAN

Truffles are impressive and a little fancy, but they're super easy to make. These little beauties are a cookies and cream cookie with cream cheese filling and a firm chocolate coating. Rolling and shaping the filling can get messy (you can wear kitchen gloves for that part), but the tasty results are so worth it!

TOOLS AND EQUIPMENT

Baking sheet

Parchment paper

Gallon-size resealable plastic bag

Rolling pin

Large mixing bowl

Silicone spatula

Medium microwave-safe bowl

Whisk

Fork

....

INGREDIENTS

24 Oreo cookies (regular, not Double Stuf)

1 (8-ounce) package cream cheese, at room temperature (see page 9)

8 ounces semisweet baking chocolate

1. Prepare the baking sheet. Line the baking sheet with parchment paper.

2. Crush the Oreos. Place the Oreo cookies in a large plastic bag, seal it, then use a rolling pin to crush the cookies. Turn the bag of cookies over and repeat on the other side. Keep going until the cookies are in small crumbs.

3. Form the truffles. Pour the crushed cookies into a large bowl and add the cream cheese. Use a spatula or your hands to mix the ingredients until you no longer see large chunks of cream cheese. Using your hands, roll the mixture into 1-inch truffle balls (you'll get about 30). Place them on the prepared baking sheet.

4. Chill the truffles. Place the baking sheet in the refrigerator for 10 to 15 minutes. This helps set the truffles and makes the chocolate coating go on more smoothly.

5. Melt the chocolate coating. A minute or so before you are ready to coat the truffles, break the chocolate into pieces and put in a medium microwave-safe bowl. Microwave for 30 seconds, whisk, then microwave again for 30 seconds, until the chocolate is melted. Whisk until smooth.

6. **Dip the truffles.** Remove the truffles from the refrigerator and use a fork to roll them one at a time in the melted chocolate, fully coating all sides. Place the coated truffles back onto the baking sheet and refrigerate for a couple of minutes, until the chocolate has set.

TRY THIS! For peppermint truffles, use mint Oreo cookies and add a drop of peppermint extract to the melted chocolate.

PB & J Crumble Bars

Makes 18 bars
Prep time: 15 minutes / Cook time: 45 minutes
NO SOY VEGETARIAN

The popular lunch box favorite flavor combo of PB & J is turned into mouth-watering snack bars. The yumminess starts with a crunchy shortbread crust, layered with swirls of peanut butter and jelly, and topped with a sweet crumb topping. So delicious!

TOOLS AND EQUIPMENT

9-by-13-inch glass baking dish

Parchment paper

2 large mixing bowls

Hand mixer

Whisk

Tablespoon

INGREDIENTS

FOR THE CRUST

1 cup (2 sticks) unsalted butter, at room temperature (see page 9)

¾ cup granulated sugar

1 teaspoon vanilla extract

2⅓ cups all-purpose flour

½ teaspoon kosher salt

FOR THE FILLING

1½ cups creamy peanut butter

1½ cups grape jelly

FOR THE CRUMB TOPPING

1 cup all-purpose flour

½ cup packed light brown sugar

1 teaspoon baking powder

½ teaspoon ground cinnamon

½ teaspoon table salt

8 tablespoons (1 stick) unsalted butter, cold

1. Preheat the oven to 350°F. Line the baking dish with parchment paper.
2. Make the crust. In a large bowl, use a hand mixer on high speed to beat the butter and sugar together until combined. Beat in the vanilla. In another large bowl, whisk together the flour and salt. Slowly add it to the butter mixture and beat until the dough starts to form a ball. Gently press the dough into the prepared baking dish, using your hands to gently even out the dough across the bottom and about ¼ inch up the sides. Wash and dry the large bowls.

Continued on next page

3. **Add the filling.** Spoon dollops of the peanut butter and jelly on top of the crust in alternating scoops a couple of inches apart. Then use the back of the spoon to smooth out the peanut butter and jelly, in a combination of streaks and swirls, to create an even layer that completely covers the crust. This ensures you get some peanut butter and some jelly in every bite!

4. **Make the crumb topping.** Combine the flour, brown sugar, baking powder, cinnamon, salt, and butter in a large bowl. Using your hands, crumble the ingredients together. You can use your thumb and index finger to squeeze the butter and crumble it in with the dry ingredients. Keep working the ingredients until you have a crumbly mixture. Sprinkle the crumb topping evenly across the peanut butter and jelly layer.

5. **Bake the cookie bars.** Place the baking dish in the oven and bake for 45 minutes. Allow to cool in the dish for 5 to 10 minutes before slicing into 18 bars.

TRY THIS! Instead of grape jelly, use strawberry, blackberry, or raspberry jam or jelly. If you're allergic to peanut butter, you can also make this recipe with soy butter or sunflower butter; it'll taste great.

Chocolate Chip Shortbread Dippers

Makes 21 cookies
Prep time: 15 minutes, plus 1 hour to chill / Cook time: 20 minutes
NO NUTS NO SOY VEGETARIAN

These soft, buttery chocolate chip shortbread cookies are dipped in melted chocolate. Cut them into small sizes for cute, compact, bite-size cookies.

TOOLS AND EQUIPMENT

Large mixing bowl

Hand mixer

Silicone spatula

Plastic wrap

Baking sheet

Parchment paper

Pastry cutter

Small microwave-safe bowl

Whisk

INGREDIENTS

1 cup (2 sticks) unsalted butter, at room temperature (see page 9)

½ teaspoon vanilla extract

⅔ cup powdered sugar

2 cups all-purpose flour

½ cup mini chocolate chips

4 ounces baking chocolate

1. **Mix the ingredients.** In a large bowl, use a hand mixer on medium speed to beat together the butter, vanilla, and powdered sugar until combined. Add the flour and mix until there are no big patches of white flour. Use a spatula to gently fold in the mini chocolate chips.

2. **Shape the dough.** Using your hands, press the dough together and shape into an 8-by-8-inch square. Wrap the dough in plastic. Refrigerate for 1 hour.

3. **Preheat the oven to 325°F.** Line the baking sheet with parchment paper. Unwrap the dough and use a pastry cutter to cut 21 equal rectangles (7 rows by 3 rows). Place the cookies on the prepared baking sheet. Leave about 1 inch of space between the cookies, as the dough will spread during baking.

4. **Bake the cookies.** Place the baking sheet in the oven and bake for 18 to 20 minutes. The edges will be light golden brown.

5. **Dip the chocolate.** Break the baking chocolate into pieces and place in a small microwave-safe bowl. Microwave for 30 seconds, whisk, then microwave again for 30 seconds, or until the chocolate is melted. Whisk until smooth. Gently dip one edge of each cookie into the chocolate. Place back on the baking sheet to cool until the chocolate is set.

Zesty Coconut Lime Macaroons

Makes about 30 cookies
Prep time: 15 minutes / Cook time: 20 minutes

NO SOY VEGETARIAN

Transport yourself to the tropics with these zesty, zingy macaroons. These little mounds of crunchy, chewy, coconutty yumminess have a bright lime flavor that tastes even more delicious when dipped in white chocolate. Be prepared to make extra, because these will disappear fast!

TOOLS AND EQUIPMENT

2 baking sheets

Parchment paper

2 large mixing bowls

Whisk

Tablespoon

Cooling rack

Medium microwave-safe bowl

Tray

INGREDIENTS

4 large egg whites

⅔ cup granulated sugar

3 tablespoons fresh lime juice

¼ teaspoon table salt

1 teaspoon vanilla extract

4½ cups unsweetened shredded coconut

½ cup all-purpose flour

8 ounces white baking chocolate

Grated lime zest (optional)

1. Preheat the oven to 325°F. Line 2 baking sheets with parchment paper.

2. Mix the ingredients. In a large bowl, whisk together the egg whites, sugar, lime juice, salt, and vanilla until the mixture is light and creamy. In another large bowl, whisk together the coconut flakes and flour. Add the wet ingredients to the dry ingredients and stir until combined.

3. Shape the cookies. Use a tablespoon to scoop out the dough and form about 30 cookie balls, then place them on the prepared baking sheets. Leave about 2 inches of space between the cookies, as the dough will spread during baking.

4. Bake the cookies. Place the baking sheets in the oven and bake for 13 to 18 minutes, until the edges start to turn a light golden brown. Allow to cool on the baking sheets for a couple of minutes before transferring to a rack to cool completely.

5. **Prepare the chocolate dip.** Break the white chocolate into pieces and put in a medium microwave-safe bowl. Microwave for 30 seconds, whisk, then microwave again for 30 seconds, until the chocolate is melted. Whisk again until smooth.

6. **Dip the baked cookies.** Line a tray with a sheet of parchment paper. Once the cookies have cooled, dip the flat bottoms of the cookies into the melted chocolate, then place them on the parchment paper. Sprinkle lime zest (if using) on top of the chocolate. Transfer to the refrigerator to set the chocolate for 2 to 5 minutes before eating.

OOPS . . . Humidity can cause macaroons to be too wet and sticky. If you live in a humid area or you're baking on a humid day, try adding 1 teaspoon cornstarch to the egg white mixture. The starch helps soak up any excess moisture caused by the humidity.

Cinnamon-Sugar Churro Sticks with Chocolate Dip

Makes 18 churro sticks

Prep time: 15 minutes, plus 30 minutes to defrost / Cook time: 10 minutes

5 INGREDIENTS OR LESS NO NUTS **NO SOY** VEGETARIAN

Churros are irresistible cinnamon-sugar desserts that are normally fried to crispy deliciousness. This recipe simplifies the traditional process by using store-bought puff pastry and baking the dough instead of frying it. The chocolate dip adds a delicious layer to these sweet treats. Make sure you pull your puff pastry out of the freezer and place it on the counter for 30 minutes before beginning this recipe.

TOOLS AND EQUIPMENT

Baking sheet

Parchment paper

Cutting board

Pastry cutter

Medium mixing bowl

Small microwave-safe bowl

Whisk

Medium microwave-safe bowl

INGREDIENTS

1 frozen puff pastry sheet, thawed (half a 1-pound package)

½ cup granulated sugar

2 teaspoons ground cinnamon

4 tablespoons (½ stick) unsalted butter

8 ounces baking chocolate or 1½ cups chocolate melting wafers

1. Preheat the oven to 450°F. Line the baking sheet with parchment paper.

2. Prepare the puff pastry. Set a cutting board on the countertop. Unfold the pastry sheet on the board. (The dough will be 9¾ inches by 10½ inches when unfolded.) Cut the dough across the longer side into 1-inch-wide strips. Then cut each strip in half, making each churro stick about 1 inch wide and 5 inches long. You should have about 18 sticks.

3. Bake the dough. Place the strips on the prepared baking sheet and bake for 10 minutes, until the dough is golden brown. Allow the churro sticks to cool for a few minutes.

Continued on next page

4. **Prepare the remaining ingredients.** Whisk together the sugar and cinnamon in a medium bowl until combined. Put the butter in a small microwave-safe bowl and melt for 45 seconds. Whisk to fully melt all the butter, then set it on the counter to cool.

5. **Make the chocolate dip.** Break the chocolate into small pieces and place in a medium microwave-safe bowl. Microwave for 30 seconds, whisk, then microwave again for 30 seconds, until the chocolate is melted. Whisk until smooth.

6. **Coat the churros.** Dip the warm (but not hot) churro strips into the melted butter and then roll in the cinnamon sugar. Serve with the melted chocolate.

TRY THIS! Add a fancy flair by twisting each puff pastry stick before baking. They come out looking like twirled breadsticks!

Mmm-Mmm Good Brownies

Makes 18 brownies
Prep time: 15 minutes / Cook time: 30 minutes
NO SOY VEGETARIAN

These rich fudge brownies are dotted with colorful, crunchy mini M&M candies. They're the perfect fix for that chocolate craving. And they're easy to pack up for a little sweet treat at lunch, for after school, or for weekend activities.

TOOLS AND EQUIPMENT

9-by-13-inch glass baking dish

Parchment paper

Large microwave-safe bowl

Whisk

Large mixing bowl

Small bowl

Silicone spatula

Toothpick

INGREDIENTS

8 tablespoons (1 stick) unsalted butter

8 ounces semisweet baking chocolate

1¼ cups granulated sugar

1 teaspoon vanilla extract

4 large eggs

½ cup plus 1 teaspoon all-purpose flour, divided

¼ teaspoon table salt

1 cup mini M&M candies

1. **Preheat the oven to 350°F.** Line the baking dish with parchment paper.

2. **Melt the butter and chocolate.** Put the butter into a large microwave-safe bowl. Break the chocolate into small pieces and add them to the bowl. Microwave for 45 seconds, whisk, then microwave again for 30 seconds, just until the ingredients have completely melted. Set it on the counter to cool.

3. **Mix the ingredients.** In a large bowl, combine the sugar, vanilla, and eggs. Whisk together until the mixture is light yellow and creamy, 3 to 4 minutes. Whisk in ½ cup of flour and the salt just until combined. Then whisk in the slightly cooled chocolate and butter mixture until all the ingredients are evenly blended.

Continued on next page

4. **Add the mini M&M's.** In a small bowl, toss the mini M&M's with the remaining 1 teaspoon of flour until well coated. This helps prevent their sinking to the bottom of the batter while baking. Use a spatula to gently fold in most of the mini M&M candies.

5. **Bake the brownies.** Pour the batter into the prepared baking dish, sprinkle the remaining mini M&M candies on top, and bake for 25 to 28 minutes, until a toothpick poked into the center comes out with a small amount of crumbs on it. The brownies will continue to firm up after they're out of the oven, so allow them to cool in the pan for 10 to 15 minutes before slicing.

DON'T HAVE IT? If you don't have mini M&M's, you can use regular M&M's or chocolate chips, or chop up some Reese's Peanut Butter Cups. You can also leave out any candy mix-ins for straight-up delicious classic fudge brownies.

TRY THIS! For another flavor layer, spoon some peanut butter on top of the brownie batter. Then use a butter knife to gently create streaks and swirls of peanut butter in the chocolate.

Chapter 4
Cakes and Cupcakes

Chocolate Lover's Double Chocolate Chip Mug Cake

Makes 1 mug cake
Prep time: 5 minutes / Cook time: 1 minute 30 seconds
REALLY FAST NO NUTS NO SOY VEGETARIAN

When you're hungry for chocolate *now*, it's mug cakes to the rescue! This recipe is a chocolate lover's dream dessert, with an easy cake batter and chocolate chips. Thanks to the microwave, you're just a few minutes away from feeding that chocolate craving.

TOOLS AND EQUIPMENT

Large or extra-large microwave-safe mug

Whisk

Fork

Toothpick

INGREDIENTS

3 tablespoons all-purpose flour

2 tablespoons granulated sugar

2 tablespoons unsweetened cocoa powder

½ teaspoon baking soda

⅛ teaspoon table salt

2 tablespoons milk

2 tablespoons vegetable oil

¼ teaspoon vanilla extract

2 tablespoons semisweet chocolate chips

1. **Mix the ingredients.** In a large or extra-large mug, whisk together the flour, sugar, cocoa powder, baking soda, and salt. Stir in the milk, oil, and vanilla. Place the chocolate chips on top, then use a fork to gently push them into the top of the batter.

2. **"Bake" the cake.** Microwave for 1 minute 30 seconds. The cake is done when you can insert a toothpick into the middle and it comes out clean. If it comes out with wet crumbs, it needs 10 to 15 more seconds in the microwave.

3. **Dig in!** Carefully remove the mug from the microwave and allow to cool down slightly before digging in.

TRY THIS! Love mint chocolate? Substitute peppermint extract for the vanilla and use chopped chocolate peppermint candies instead of chocolate chips.

Snickerdoodle Snacking Cake

Makes 16 servings
Prep time: 10 minutes / Cook time: 30 minutes
REALLY FAST **NO NUTS** **NO SOY** VEGETARIAN

The cinnamon-sugar goodness of snickerdoodle cookies makes its way into a light and fluffy cake. This is a simple, easy recipe that delivers big snack flavors. For an added layer of yumminess, top the cake with the cream cheese frosting from Microwave Mini Carrot Cakes (page 66).

TOOLS AND EQUIPMENT

8-by-8-inch square baking pan

Parchment paper

Small microwave-safe bowl

Whisk

Large mixing bowl

Small mixing bowl

Knife

....

INGREDIENTS

FOR THE CAKE

4 tablespoons (½ stick) unsalted butter

1 cup all-purpose flour

1 cup granulated sugar

1 teaspoon ground cinnamon

2 teaspoons baking powder

½ cup milk

1 large egg

FOR THE TOPPING

1 tablespoon granulated sugar

¼ teaspoon ground cinnamon

1. **Preheat the oven to 400°F.** Line the baking pan with parchment paper.

2. **Melt the butter.** Place the butter in a small microwave-safe bowl and melt for 45 seconds. Whisk to fully melt all the butter. Set it aside to cool.

3. **Mix the ingredients.** In a large bowl, whisk together the flour, sugar, cinnamon, and baking powder. Then whisk in the milk, followed by the egg, then the melted butter. Pour the batter into the prepared baking pan.

4. **Add the topping.** In a small bowl, mix the sugar and cinnamon. Sprinkle the cinnamon sugar evenly over the top of the cake.

5. **Bake the cake.** Place the baking pan in the oven and bake for 25 to 30 minutes. Allow to cool for 10 minutes in the pan before slicing into squares.

Peppermint Mocha Lava Cake

Makes 6 cakes
Prep time: 10 minutes / Cook time: 20 minutes
REALLY FAST   NO NUTS   **NO SOY**   VEGETARIAN

This decadent dessert has layers of flavors, and you'll love the ooey-gooey filling in the middle. For extra chocolate flavor, drizzle some chocolate ganache on top of each cake after it's baked (find instructions for the ganache in S'mores Campfire Cupcakes on page 73). If you don't have ramekins, divide the batter among 6 cups of a standard muffin pan.

TOOLS AND EQUIPMENT

Medium microwave-safe bowl

Whisk

6 (6- to 8-ounce) ramekins

Large mixing bowl

Baking sheet

....

INGREDIENTS

4 ounces semisweet baking chocolate

8 tablespoons (1 stick) unsalted

butter, plus more for greasing

Unsweetened cocoa powder, for dusting

3 large eggs

½ cup granulated sugar

¼ cup all-purpose flour

1 teaspoon vanilla extract

½ teaspoon peppermint extract

½ teaspoon instant coffee powder

1. Melt the chocolate and butter. Break the chocolate into small pieces and put in a medium microwave-safe bowl. Add the butter. Microwave for 45 seconds, whisk, then microwave for 30 seconds more, or until the mixture is just melted. Set it aside to cool.

2. Preheat the oven to 400°F. Grease the insides of 6 ramekins with some butter, then dust with some cocoa powder.

3. Mix the ingredients. In a large bowl, whisk the eggs and sugar together until creamy. Whisk in the melted chocolate and butter. Then whisk in the flour, vanilla and peppermint extracts, and instant coffee.

4. Bake the cakes. Pour the batter into the prepared ramekins until just over half full. Place the ramekins on a baking sheet. Bake for 12 to 17 minutes. The cakes are done when the edges start to pull away from the ramekins; the centers will still be jiggly. Let cool briefly, then enjoy.

Dreamy Mint Chocolate Chip Icebox Cake

Makes 10 to 12 servings

Prep time: 10 minutes, plus 1 hour to freeze

5 INGREDIENTS OR LESS NO HEAT NECESSARY NO NUTS NO SOY VEGETARIAN

Icebox cakes have been around for generations. They are popular because they give you lots of flavor for very little effort. This frozen treat is a mint chocolate chip lover's dream. My family has been known to dive in with spoons and eat this cake directly from the pan, but you can slice the cake into squares if you're feeling more civilized.

TOOLS AND EQUIPMENT

8-by-8-inch baking pan

Plastic wrap

Large mixing bowl

Whisk

Silicone spatula

Offset spatula

INGREDIENTS

1 (8-ounce) container frozen whipped topping, thawed

½ teaspoon peppermint extract

¼ cup granulated sugar

1 or 2 drops green food coloring (optional)

½ cup mini chocolate chips

30 thin chocolate wafer cookies

1. **Prepare the pan.** Line the bottom and sides of the baking pan with plastic wrap.

2. **Make the filling.** In a large bowl, whisk together the whipped topping, peppermint extract, sugar, and green food coloring (if using), until the ingredients are well combined and the food coloring is evenly distributed. Using a spatula, gently fold in the mini chocolate chips.

3. **Assemble the cake.** Arrange 9 chocolate wafer cookies on the bottom of the baking pan. Crush a couple more cookies with your hands and use those to fill in any cracks between the whole cookies. Using an offset spatula, spread one-third of the filling over the cookies, extending it to the edges and into the corners. Place another layer of 9 cookies over the filling, then top with one-third more of the filling. Place the final 9 cookies on top, then add the remaining filling. Use the spatula to smooth the top.

Continued on next page

4. **Chill the cake.** Cover the pan with plastic wrap and freeze for at least 1 hour, until the filling is solid to the touch. Keep the cake frozen until you are ready to eat.

5. **Serve the cake.** Remove the plastic wrap and carefully remove the cake from the pan. Place the cake on a plate, then slice and serve.

DON'T HAVE IT? If you can't find thin chocolate wafer cookies, you can use Oreos; it's just as delicious! Just be sure to break the cookies into smaller pieces and sprinkle the crumbs instead of laying the cookies flat. This makes the cake easier to slice and eat when frozen.

TRY THIS! Feel free to experiment using similar measurements to create other icebox cake flavors. To create a strawberry icebox cake, use vanilla extract instead of peppermint and fold fresh strawberry slices into the whipped filling instead of mini chocolate chips. To create a peanut butter chip icebox cake, use vanilla extract instead of peppermint and fold in ½ cup creamy peanut butter along with the mini chocolate chips.

One-Bowl Olive Oil Cake

Makes 8 servings
Prep time: 10 minutes / Cook time: 35 minutes

REALLY FAST **NO SOY** VEGETARIAN

This delicious olive oil cake is slightly denser than a layer cake, and it's so easy to make: you just mix all the ingredients in one bowl. The flavors are sophisticated and grown-up, but it's still so much fun to eat!

TOOLS AND EQUIPMENT

9-inch round cake pan

Parchment paper

Large mixing bowl

Whisk

Cooling rack

Pastry brush

INGREDIENTS

3 large eggs

1 cup granulated sugar

1 cup extra-virgin olive oil, plus more for brushing

½ cup milk

½ teaspoon vanilla extract

½ teaspoon almond extract

1½ cups all-purpose flour

1 teaspoon baking powder

½ teaspoon baking soda

¼ teaspoon table salt

1. **Preheat the oven to 350°F.** Line the cake pan with parchment paper.

2. **Mix the ingredients.** In a large bowl, whisk together the eggs and sugar until light and fluffy, about 2 minutes. Slowly whisk in the olive oil, milk, and vanilla and almond extracts. Add the flour, baking powder, baking soda, and salt and slowly whisk the dry ingredients into the wet ingredients until just combined. Pour the batter into the prepared pan.

3. **Bake the cake.** Place the pan in the oven and bake for 30 to 35 minutes. Allow the cake to cool in the pan for 5 minutes, then transfer to a rack to cool completely. Just before serving, use a pastry brush to brush a thin layer of olive oil on top of the cake.

SWITCH IT UP! Make this a lemon poppyseed cake by substituting lemon extract and lemon zest for the almond extract and sprinkling 1 tablespoon poppy seeds into the batter.

Blackberry Cheesecake Squares

Serves 8 to 10

Prep time: 10 minutes, plus 1 hour to chill / Cook time: 35 minutes

NO NUTS NO SOY VEGETARIAN

These cheesecake squares make great after-school snacks, or snacks for hungry teammates after practice. You can keep them in the refrigerator for up to five days, or in the freezer for up to one month. Just set them out on the counter to thaw for several minutes if you've frozen them.

TOOLS AND EQUIPMENT

8-inch square baking pan

Parchment paper

Large microwave-safe bowl

Whisk

Large resealable plastic bag

Rolling pin

Silicone spatula

Large mixing bowl

Hand mixer

Tablespoon

Aluminum foil or plastic wrap

Knife

INGREDIENTS

FOR THE CRUST

6 tablespoons (¾ stick) unsalted butter

9 whole graham crackers

⅓ cup granulated sugar

FOR THE FILLING

2 (8-ounce) packages cream cheese, at room temperature (see page 9)

1 large egg

⅓ cup granulated sugar

½ cup fresh lemon juice

½ teaspoon vanilla extract

1½ cups fresh or frozen blackberries

1. **Preheat the oven to 350°F.** Line the baking pan with parchment paper, with some of the paper overhanging the sides of the pan.

2. **Melt the butter.** Place the butter in a large microwave-safe bowl and melt for 45 seconds, then whisk to fully melt all the butter. Set it on the counter to cool.

3. **Make the crust.** Place the graham crackers in a large plastic bag, seal, and use a rolling pin to crush the crackers into small crumbs. Pour the crumbs into the bowl with the melted butter, then add the sugar and use a spatula to mix well. Press the mixture into the bottom and slightly up the sides of the prepared pan. Bake for 5 minutes. Allow to cool while you wash and dry the spatula and prepare the filling.

4. **Make the filling.** In a large bowl, use a hand mixer on medium speed to beat the cream cheese until smooth, about 1 minute. Next, beat in the egg, sugar, lemon juice, and vanilla until smooth and creamy, 3 to 4 minutes. Using the spatula, gently fold in the blackberries. The color from the blackberries will swirl in the batter; this is normal, and it creates a nice colorful pattern in the cheesecake squares. Spoon the filling onto the crust and smooth out the top with the bottom of the spoon.

5. **Bake the cheesecake.** Place the baking pan in the oven and bake for 30 to 35 minutes. The cheesecake is done when the edges are lightly browned. It's okay if the center isn't firm, but it shouldn't be liquid-y. Allow the cheesecake to cool in the pan at room temperature for 30 minutes, then cover with aluminum foil or plastic wrap and chill in the refrigerator for at least 1 hour.

6. **Serve.** Once the cheesecake has set and the center is firm, lift the parchment paper out of the pan, fold down the paper, and cut the cheesecake into squares.

DON'T HAVE IT? If you don't have graham crackers, you can use Biscoff cookies or gingersnap cookies instead. Or, you can make a shortbread crust using the crust ingredients and instructions from Melt-in-Your-Mouth Lemon Bars (page 34).

TRY THIS! These cheesecake squares are great made with almost any berry. Try blueberries, strawberries, or raspberries, or even pitted cherries to mix things up. You can also add grated lemon zest for a stronger lemon flavor.

No-Bake Mango Lime Cheesecake

Serves 8 to 10

Prep time: 15 minutes, plus at least 2 hours to chill

NO NUTS **NO SOY** VEGETARIAN

Too hot to turn on the oven? Try this no-bake cheesecake. With tropical mango and zesty lime, it's packed with big fruit flavors—a tasty way to cool off on a hot day! This is a great cheesecake to make ahead; it can be frozen for up to one month before being served. To serve a frozen cheesecake, remove it from the freezer and thaw at room temperature for at least one hour.

TOOLS AND EQUIPMENT

Large microwave-safe bowl

Whisk

Large resealable plastic bag

Rolling pin

Silicone spatula

9-inch nonstick springform pan

Cutting board

Knife

Large mixing bowl

Hand mixer

INGREDIENTS

FOR THE CRUST

4 tablespoons (½ stick) unsalted butter

10 whole graham crackers

2 tablespoons granulated sugar

2 teaspoons vanilla extract

FOR THE FILLING

1½ cups frozen mango chunks, thawed

2 (8-ounce) packages full-fat cream cheese, at room temperature (see page 9)

1 (14-ounce) can full-fat sweetened condensed milk

1½ cups granulated sugar

½ cup fresh lime juice

1 (8-ounce) tub frozen whipped topping, thawed

Grated zest of 1 lime, for garnish (optional)

1. **Make the crust.** Put the butter in a large microwave-safe bowl and melt for 45 seconds. Whisk to fully melt all the butter, then set it on the counter to cool. Put the graham crackers in a large plastic bag, seal, and use a rolling pin to crush the crackers into small crumbs. Add the crushed crackers to the bowl with the butter, then whisk in the sugar and vanilla until the ingredients are well combined. Use a spatula to press the crust down into the bottom and about ½ inch up the sides of a nonstick springform pan.

2. **Make the filling.** On a cutting board, use a knife to dice the mango into smaller pieces. In a large bowl and using a hand mixer on medium speed, beat the cream cheese until creamy and smooth. This step is important in helping your cheesecake set properly. Once the cream cheese is smooth, turn the mixer to low speed and beat in the condensed milk, sugar, and lime juice. Add the mango to the bowl and use the spatula to fold all the ingredients together until they are evenly combined. Pour the filling over the crust. Top with an even layer of whipped topping.

3. **Chill the cheesecake.** Refrigerate the cheesecake for at least 2 hours and up to overnight. When it's ready, it will be firm all the way through.

4. **Garnish (optional).** For extra flavor and decoration, sprinkle the lime zest over the top.

OOPS . . . Is your cheesecake still runny after a few hours in the refrigerator? This can happen if you use lower-fat cream cheese or lower-fat condensed milk, or if the cream cheese isn't beaten well. If your filling isn't setting after 2 to 3 hours in the refrigerator, you can freeze it.

Microwave Mini Carrot Cakes with Cream Cheese Frosting

Makes 4 mini cakes
Prep time: 15 minutes / Cook time: 5 minutes
NO NUTS **NO SOY** VEGETARIAN

What's better than carrot cake? Your own individual carrot cake! These are moist and fluffy, are full of delicious spices, and have a sweet cream cheese frosting that works equally well with other cake and cupcake recipes in this book, such as Snickerdoodle Snacking Cake (page 57) and Gingerbread Spice Muffins (page 21).

TOOLS AND EQUIPMENT

4 microwave-safe 8-ounce ramekins

Large microwave-safe bowl

Whisk

Vegetable peeler

Box grater

Toothpick

Medium microwave-safe bowl

Butter knife

Cutting board

Knife

Offset spatula

....

INGREDIENTS

FOR THE CAKES

2 tablespoons unsalted butter, plus more for greasing

1 large carrot

1 large egg

¼ cup packed light brown sugar

¼ cup milk

1 tablespoon vegetable oil

½ teaspoon vanilla extract

½ cup all-purpose flour

1 teaspoon ground cinnamon

¼ teaspoon ground nutmeg

¼ teaspoon baking soda

½ teaspoon baking powder

¼ teaspoon table salt

FOR THE CREAM CHEESE FROSTING

½ cup (4 ounces) cream cheese

1 tablespoon unsalted butter, at room temperature (see page 9)

1 teaspoon vanilla extract

1¼ cups powdered sugar

1. **Prep the ramekins and ingredients.** Grease the insides of the ramekins with some butter. Place the 2 tablespoons butter in a large microwave-safe bowl and microwave for 30 seconds. Whisk until smooth. Peel and finely shred the carrot using a box grater; you should have ½ cup. Add the shredded carrot to the bowl with the melted butter.

2. **Mix the ingredients.** Whisk the egg, brown sugar, milk, oil, and vanilla into the bowl with the butter and carrot until well combined. Then whisk in the flour, cinnamon, nutmeg, baking soda, baking powder, and salt.

3. **Microwave the cakes.** Pour an equal amount of the batter into the ramekins, filling each about half full. Microwave for 1 minute, then for 30 seconds more at a time until a toothpick inserted into the center of one cake comes out clean, between 2 minutes 30 seconds and 3 minutes total. The ramekins will be hot, so use oven mitts to carefully remove them from the microwave. Allow them to cool for a minute or so at room temperature.

4. **Make the cream cheese frosting.** While the cakes are cooling, put the cream cheese in a medium microwave-safe bowl and microwave for 15 seconds. Remove from the microwave and whisk in the butter, vanilla, and powdered sugar until well combined.

5. **Cut and frost the cakes.** When the cakes have cooled to the touch, run a butter knife along the inside edge of each ramekin to release them, then invert and place them on a cutting board. Slice each cake in half horizontally and use an offset spatula to spread 1 to 2 tablespoons of frosting between the layers. Top each cake with the remaining frosting.

DON'T HAVE IT? If you don't have 8-ounce ramekins, you can make these in large microwave-safe mugs. Just be sure the mugs are 8-ounce mugs with tall sides that allow the cakes to rise without overflowing.

Strawberries and Cream Cupcakes

Makes 24 cupcakes
Prep time: 20 minutes / Cook time: 20 minutes

NO NUTS **NO SOY** VEGETARIAN

Compared with other baked goods, cupcakes can take a little more time to make, but they're so worth it. This recipe shortens the process by fancying up some store-bought cake mix and frosting, so most of the prep time is spent assembling the cupcakes. You can also cut out the filling completely if you wish—the cupcakes are just as delicious without!

TOOLS AND EQUIPMENT

2 (12-cup) muffin pans

24 cupcake liners

Large mixing bowl

Whisk

Toothpick

Cooling rack

Hand mixer

Silicone spatula

Teaspoon

Tablespoon

Medium mixing bowl

Offset spatula

Large resealable plastic bag and scissors (optional)

....

INGREDIENTS

FOR THE CAKE

1 (15.25-ounce) box strawberry cake mix

2 large eggs

½ cup vegetable oil

FOR THE FILLING

1 (3-ounce) package cream cheese, at room temperature (see page 9)

¼ cup heavy (whipping) cream

¼ cup powdered sugar

½ teaspoon vanilla extract

¼ cup diced fresh strawberries

FOR THE FROSTING

¼ cup diced fresh strawberries

1 (16-ounce) can cream cheese frosting

1. Preheat the oven to 350°F. Line 2 muffin pans with the cupcake liners.

2. **Mix the cupcake ingredients.** In a large bowl, whisk together the cake mix, eggs, and oil.

3. **Bake the cupcakes.** Pour the batter into the prepared muffin cups, filling each just more than halfway. Bake for 15 to 17 minutes, or until a toothpick inserted into the middle of a cupcake comes out clean. Set the pan on a rack to cool completely. Wash and dry the large bowl.

4. **Make the filling.** In the large bowl, use a hand mixer on medium speed to beat the cream cheese until smooth. Then beat in the heavy cream, powdered sugar, and vanilla. Finally, use a spatula to fold in the diced strawberries. Once the cupcakes have cooled completely, use a teaspoon to carefully scoop out a small circle in the center of each cupcake from the top, almost halfway down (don't scoop through the bottom of the cupcake or the filling will fall out). Spoon about 1 tablespoon of filling into each hole. Wash and dry the spatula.

5. **Make the frosting.** In a medium bowl, use the spatula to fold the strawberries into the cream cheese frosting. Using an offset spatula, frost the top of each cupcake. Or, spoon the frosting into a plastic bag, cut across one bottom corner of the bag to make a small hole, and squeeze the bag to push the frosting out to top each cupcake.

SWITCH IT UP! Turn this recipe into a two-layer cake by baking the cupcake ingredients in two 9-inch round baking pans and adding an extra 5 to 7 minutes of baking time. Double the measurements for the filling ingredients and use it to fill between the two layers. Then use an offset spatula to spread the frosting on top of the cake.

Pumpkin Spice Cupcakes

Makes 24 cupcakes
Prep time: 20 minutes / Cook time: 25 minutes

NO NUTS **NO SOY** VEGETARIAN

Although the flavors of these cupcakes are popular each fall, in our house we love to make them any time of the year. They're always a hit with friends and family, too. The cupcakes are wonderfully moist, and the frosting has a touch of cinnamon for final flavor. Your house will smell amazing while these are baking!

TOOLS AND EQUIPMENT

2 (12-cup) muffin pans

24 cupcake liners

2 large mixing bowls

Hand mixer

Whisk

Toothpick

Cooling rack

Offset spatula

INGREDIENTS

FOR THE CUPCAKES

¾ cup (1½ sticks) unsalted butter, at room temperature (see page 9)

2 cups granulated sugar

3 large eggs

½ cup vegetable oil

1 (15-ounce) can pumpkin puree

2⅓ cups all-purpose flour

1 tablespoon pumpkin pie spice

1 teaspoon baking powder

½ teaspoon baking soda

¼ teaspoon table salt

FOR THE FROSTING

1 (8-ounce) package cream cheese, at room temperature (see page 9)

8 tablespoons (1 stick) unsalted butter, at room temperature (see page 9)

3 cups powdered sugar

1 teaspoon vanilla extract

½ teaspoon ground cinnamon

1. **Preheat the oven to 350°F.** Line 2 muffin pans with the cupcake liners.

2. **Mix the ingredients.** In a large bowl, use a hand mixer on high speed to beat together the butter and sugar until light and fluffy. Beat in the eggs one at a time, then add the oil and pumpkin puree. In another large bowl, whisk together the flour, pumpkin pie spice, baking powder, baking soda, and salt. Gradually whisk the dry mixture into the wet mixture.

3. **Bake the cupcakes.** Pour the batter into the prepared muffin pan, filling each cup about three-fourths full. Bake for 20 to 25 minutes, or until a toothpick inserted into the center of a cupcake comes out clean. Allow the cupcakes to cool in the pan for 10 minutes, then transfer to a rack to cool completely.

4. **Make the frosting.** Wash and dry the beaters of the mixer and the mixing bowls. In a large bowl, use the hand mixer on medium speed to beat together the cream cheese and butter until light and fluffy. Slowly beat in the powdered sugar, vanilla, and cinnamon. Use an offset spatula to frost the top of each cupcake.

DON'T HAVE IT? If you don't have pumpkin pie spice, you can make your own! In a medium bowl, whisk together 1 tablespoon ground cinnamon, 2 teaspoons ground ginger, ½ teaspoon ground allspice, ½ teaspoon ground cloves, and ½ teaspoon ground nutmeg. You can also use your homemade pumpkin spice to top whipped cream on hot cocoa. So yummy!

TRY THIS! Top each cupcake with a sprinkling of chopped pecans or walnuts for some crunch.

S'mores Campfire Cupcakes with Chocolate Ganache and Toasty Marshmallows

Makes 24 cupcakes
Prep time: 20 minutes / Cook time: 25 minutes
NO NUTS NO SOY VEGETARIAN

Enjoy the delicious flavors of s'mores without the campfire mess. These fun cupcakes have a graham cracker base, a rich chocolate cake, and a topping of chocolate ganache and toasty marshmallows.

TOOLS AND EQUIPMENT

2 (12-cup) muffin pans

24 cupcake liners

2 large mixing bowls

Hand mixer

Whisk

Toothpick

Medium microwave-safe bowl

Cooling rack

Baking sheet

Aluminum foil

....

INGREDIENTS

FOR THE CRUST

3 whole graham crackers

FOR THE CUPCAKES

2 cups granulated sugar

½ cup vegetable oil

1 cup sour cream

2 teaspoons vanilla extract

2 large eggs

2 cups all-purpose flour

1 cup unsweetened cocoa powder

2 teaspoons baking powder

1 teaspoon baking soda

½ teaspoon table salt

½ cup milk

FOR THE CHOCO-LATE GANACHE

8 ounces semisweet baking chocolate

2 tablespoons heavy (whipping) cream

FOR THE MARSHMALLOWS

Nonstick cooking spray

24 marshmallows

1. Preheat the oven to 350°F. Line 2 muffin pans with the cupcake liners.

2. Lay in the graham cracker "crust." Snap each graham cracker into fourths, then snap those fourths in half, into 8 small squares. Place one square on the bottom of each prepared cupcake cup.

Continued on next page

3. **Make the batter.** In a large bowl, use a hand mixer on low speed to beat together the sugar and oil until fluffy, about 1 minute. Beat in the sour cream and vanilla, then beat in the eggs one at a time. In another large bowl, whisk together the flour, cocoa powder, baking powder, baking soda, and salt. Slowly whisk the dry mixture into the wet mixture, then whisk in the milk until fully combined.

4. **Bake the cupcakes.** Pour the batter on top of the graham cracker squares in the cupcake cups, filling each to just over halfway, leaving space for the batter to rise. Bake for 20 to 25 minutes, or until a toothpick inserted into the center of a cupcake comes out clean. Allow the cupcakes to cool in the pans for 10 minutes. Turn the oven to broil.

5. **Make the chocolate ganache.** In a medium microwave-safe bowl, break the chocolate into small pieces and pour in the heavy cream. Microwave for 30 seconds. Whisk, then microwave again for 30 seconds, until both are melted. Whisk until smooth. Gently dip the top of each cupcake into the chocolate ganache, coating the top of the cupcakes evenly. Place on a rack to set.

6. **"Toast" the marshmallows.** Line a baking sheet with aluminum foil and spray lightly with nonstick cooking spray. Place the marshmallows in a single layer on the foil and broil for 2 to 3 minutes. Watch them carefully through the oven window and take them out just when the tops start to turn a toasty brown. Top each cupcake with a marshmallow.

OOPS . . . Did your chocolate harden while it was melting in the microwave, or after melting? You can "wake up" chocolate that has seized up like this by pouring 1 tablespoon boiling water into the chocolate and then whisking it smooth. If needed, add more boiling water 1 tablespoon at a time and whisk until the chocolate is shiny, wet, and smooth.

Classic Chocolate Sheet Cake with Chocolate Frosting

Serves 12 to 15

Prep time: 15 minutes, plus 20 minutes to chill / Cook time: 25 minutes

NO NUTS NO SOY VEGETARIAN

A classic chocolate sheet cake never goes out of style and is so versatile. This is a great cake to make when you're feeding a crowd, because it's one layer that can be cut into a dozen square slices . . . or many more, depending on size. Our family uses large cookie cutters to cut out fun shapes for the holidays, and we decorate the cake with colored cream cheese frosting from Microwave Mini Carrot Cakes (page 66) and sprinkles.

TOOLS AND EQUIPMENT

13-by-18-inch rimmed baking sheet

Parchment paper

2 large mixing bowls

Whisk

Medium microwave-safe bowl

Offset spatula

Toothpick

Cooling rack

Hand mixer

....

INGREDIENTS

FOR THE CAKE

2 cups all-purpose flour

1 cup granulated sugar

1 teaspoon baking soda

¼ teaspoon table salt

½ cup buttermilk

½ cup plain Greek yogurt

1 teaspoon vanilla extract

2 large eggs

1 cup (2 sticks) unsalted butter

¼ cup unsweetened cocoa powder

FOR THE CHOCOLATE FROSTING

1 cup (2 sticks) unsalted butter, at room temperature (see page 9)

½ teaspoon table salt

¾ cup unsweetened cocoa powder

2 teaspoons vanilla extract

2½ cups powdered sugar

¼ cup heavy cream

1. **Preheat the oven to 350°F.** Line the baking sheet with parchment paper.

2. **Mix the dry ingredients.** In a large bowl, whisk together the flour, granulated sugar, baking soda, and salt.

Continued on next page

3. **Mix the wet ingredients.** In another large bowl, whisk together the buttermilk, yogurt, and vanilla. Then whisk in the eggs, one at a time.

4. **Melt the butter.** Put the butter in a medium microwave-safe bowl and melt for 45 seconds. Whisk to fully melt all the butter. Add the cocoa powder to the melted butter and whisk until smooth.

5. **Combine the mixtures to make the batter.** Pour the chocolate-butter mixture into the bowl with the dry ingredients and whisk together. Then whisk this mixture slowly into the bowl with the wet ingredients. Stir everything together until smooth.

6. **Bake the cake.** Pour the batter into the prepared pan, using an offset spatula to spread the batter evenly into the sides and corners. Bake for 20 to 25 minutes, or until a toothpick inserted in the center comes out clean. Place the pan on a rack for the cake to cool in the pan at room temperature. Wash and dry the mixing bowls.

7. **Make the frosting.** In one of the large bowls, use a hand mixer on low speed to beat the butter and salt until smooth and creamy. Gradually add the cocoa powder, then the vanilla. Beat the powdered sugar into the mixture 1 cup at a time, then beat in the heavy cream. Increase the speed to medium and beat the mixture for 1 minute, until light and airy. Use the offset spatula to frost the cake. Chill in the refrigerator for 20 minutes before slicing.

TRY THIS! Cut the cake into 2 equal squares to make a layer cake and frost the top and between the layers with either the chocolate frosting in this recipe or Cream Cheese Frosting (page 66).

Pineapple Poke Cake

Serves 10 to 12

Prep time: 10 minutes, plus 1 hour to chill / Cook time: 30 minutes

NO SOY VEGETARIAN

This cake is bursting with sweet tropical flavors that remind me of cakes we'd eat on family vacations in Hawaii. The shredded coconut adds a nice light crunch to balance the moist cake. Keep this cake refrigerated so the whipped topping stays cold.

TOOLS AND EQUIPMENT

9-by-13-inch glass baking dish

Parchment paper

Large mixing bowl

Whisk

Toothpick

Medium microwave-safe bowl

Straw or fork

Offset spatula

INGREDIENTS

1 (15.25-ounce) box yellow cake mix

2 large eggs

⅓ cup vegetable oil

1¼ cups water

1 cup milk

1 (1-ounce) package instant vanilla pudding mix

1 (8-ounce) can crushed pineapple

¼ cup packed light brown sugar

1 (8-ounce) tub frozen whipped topping, thawed

½ cup unsweetened shredded coconut

1. **Preheat the oven to 350°F.** Line the baking dish with parchment paper.

2. **Mix the ingredients.** In a large bowl, whisk together the cake mix, eggs, oil, water, milk, and pudding mix. Pour the batter into the prepared dish.

3. **Bake the cake.** Place the baking dish in the oven and bake for 25 to 30 minutes, until a toothpick inserted in the center comes out clean.

4. **Make the pineapple flavoring.** While the cake is baking, put the pineapple and brown sugar in a medium microwave-safe bowl. Microwave for 45 seconds, then whisk until smooth.

5. **Poke the cake.** When the cake is done, poke holes in the top with a straw or large fork. Pour the pineapple mixture over the top of the cake so it drips down into the holes into the cake. Refrigerate the cake to chill completely, at least 1 hour. Once cold, use a spatula to top the cake with the whipped topping, then sprinkle with the shredded coconut.

Sugar Cookie Confetti Cake

Serves 8 to 10

Prep time: 10 minutes / Cook time: 30 minutes

REALLY FAST NO NUTS NO SOY VEGETARIAN

Two delicious desserts collide in this sweet, colorful cookie-cake hybrid. Just like a cookie, the center is chewy, and just like a cake, you can slice it to serve a crowd. The sprinkles and white chocolate chips help make it super fun and festive. We've served this at my daughter's birthday, as well as times when just having friends over; whenever we have it, there are never any leftovers.

TOOLS AND EQUIPMENT

9-inch pie pan

Parchment paper

2 large mixing bowls

Hand mixer

Whisk

Silicone spatula

Cooling rack

Knife

INGREDIENTS

8 tablespoons (1 stick) unsalted butter, at room temperature (see page 9)

¾ cup granulated sugar

1 large egg

1 tablespoon vanilla extract

1½ cups all-purpose flour

¼ teaspoon table salt

1 teaspoon baking powder

½ teaspoon baking soda

½ teaspoon cream of tartar

½ cup white chocolate chips

¼ cup rainbow sprinkles

1. **Preheat the oven to 350°F.** Line the pie pan with parchment paper, with a little overhang on the edges.

2. **Mix the wet ingredients.** In a large bowl, use a hand mixer on medium speed to cream the butter and sugar until light and fluffy, about 1 minute. Beat in the egg and vanilla.

3. **Mix the dry ingredients.** In another large bowl, whisk together the flour, salt, baking powder, baking soda, and cream of tartar.

4. **Combine the ingredients.** Slowly add the dry ingredients to the wet ingredients, stirring to combine using a spatula. The dough will be thick, like cookie dough. Use the spatula to gently fold in the chocolate chips and sprinkles.

Continued on next page

5. **Bake the cookie cake.** Press the cookie dough evenly into the prepared pie pan. Bake for 25 to 30 minutes, or until the center is still slightly soft but the edges and top are a light golden brown. Do not wait until the center is firm, or you will overbake the cake. Lift the cake out of the pie pan by gripping the parchment paper, then transfer it to a rack to cool completely. Slice and serve.

DON'T HAVE IT? If you don't have cream of tartar, you can use ½ teaspoon more baking powder. Or, you can simply leave it out. In this recipe, the cream of tartar acts to make the batter fluffier. If you leave it out, the cake will have a slightly thicker texture, more like a cookie, but it will still taste absolutely delicious.

TRY THIS! Frost the cookie cake using the Cream Cheese Frosting on page 66. Use an offset spatula to spread the frosting over the top of the cake before slicing. Or, spoon the frosting into a plastic bag, cut across one bottom corner of the bag to make a small hole, and squeeze the bag to push the frosting out to pipe it along the edge of the top of the cake and center of the cake in any pattern you wish. You could even use the frosting to spell out a birthday greeting on the cake!

Cookies and Cream Cupcakes

Makes 24 cupcakes
Prep time: 20 minutes / Cook time: 25 minutes
NO NUTS NO SOY VEGETARIAN

Cookies and cream have always been at the top of the flavor-combo pile for both of my teens. These cupcakes are loaded with cookies and cream, both in the cupcakes and in the frosting. We love making these for birthdays—they're so fun and festive!

TOOLS AND EQUIPMENT

2 (12-cup) muffin pans

24 cupcake liners

Large resealable plastic bag (or 2 with scissors; optional)

Rolling pin

2 large mixing bowls

Whisk

Hand mixer

Silicone spatula

Toothpick

Offset spatula

INGREDIENTS

FOR THE CUPCAKES

30 Oreo cookies, plus extra cookies cut in half, for garnish

1 cup granulated sugar

¼ cup packed light brown sugar

½ cup vegetable oil

1 tablespoon vanilla extract

3 large eggs

⅓ cup sour cream

2½ cups all-purpose flour

3 teaspoons baking powder

½ teaspoon table salt

1 cup milk

FOR THE COOKIES AND CREAM FROSTING

1 (8-ounce) package cream cheese, at room temperature (see page 9)

8 tablespoons (1 stick) unsalted butter, at room temperature (see page 9)

3 cups powdered sugar

1 teaspoon vanilla extract

1. **Preheat the oven to 350°F.** Line 2 muffin pans with the cupcake liners.

2. **Crush the cookies.** Place the Oreos in a large plastic bag, seal, and use a rolling pin to crush them into small crumbs. You should end up with 2 to 2½ cups of crushed cookies.

3. **Mix the wet ingredients.** In a large bowl, whisk together the granulated sugar, brown sugar, oil, and vanilla. Then whisk in the eggs one at a time. Whisk in the sour cream until combined.

Continued on next page

4. **Mix the dry ingredients.** In another large bowl, whisk together the flour, baking powder, and salt.

5. **Make the batter.** Using a hand mixer on low speed, gradually alternate between adding some of the dry ingredients to the wet ingredients, then some of the milk to the wet ingredients. Continue mixing until all the ingredients are combined. Use a spatula to gently fold in 1 cup of the crushed cookies. (Save the rest for the frosting.)

6. **Bake the cupcakes.** Pour the batter into the prepared muffin pans, filling each cup about three-fourths full. Place the muffin pans in the oven and bake for 20 to 25 minutes, or until a toothpick inserted into the center of a cupcake comes out clean. Allow the cupcakes to cool in the pans completely. Wash and dry the beaters of the hand mixer and the mixing bowls.

7. **Make the frosting.** In a large bowl, use the hand mixer on medium speed to beat the cream cheese until smooth, about 1 minute. Add the butter and beat together for 1 more minute. Turn the mixer to low speed and slowly mix in the powdered sugar and vanilla. Using the spatula, gently fold in the remaining crushed cookies.

8. **Decorate the cupcakes.** Frost the cupcakes using the offset spatula. Or, spoon the frosting into a plastic bag, cut across one bottom corner of the bag to make a small hole, and squeeze the bag to push the frosting out to frost each cupcake. For extra garnish, place half an Oreo on top of each cupcake.

TRY THIS! Use Chocolate Frosting (page 75) or Cream Cheese Frosting (page 66) instead of the Cookies and Cream Frosting.

Chapter 5
Pies and Tarts

Sweet Summer Fruit Galette

Serves 8

Prep time: 15 minutes / Cook time: 25 minutes

NO NUTS **NO SOY** VEGETARIAN

A galette (also known as a crostata) is a simple free-form, rustic pie that's usually sweet but can also be savory. This recipe celebrates summer's best fruits. My family loves to make this galette using a combination of fresh berries that we have picked from local farms.

TOOLS AND EQUIPMENT

Baking sheet

Parchment paper

2 small bowls

Medium mixing bowl

Tablespoon

Cutting board

Knife

Fork

Pastry brush

Cooling rack

....

INGREDIENTS

1 refrigerated pie crust, at room temperature

½ cup plus 2 tablespoons granulated sugar, divided

1¼ teaspoons ground cinnamon, divided

1 (14.5-ounce) can sliced peaches

1 pint fresh raspberries

2 tablespoons cornstarch

2 teaspoons fresh lemon juice

1 tablespoon cold unsalted butter

1 large egg

1. **Preheat the oven to 425°F.** Line the baking sheet with parchment paper. Unroll the pie crust and place it on the prepared baking sheet.

2. **Make the cinnamon sugar topping.** In a small bowl, combine 2 tablespoons of the sugar with ¼ teaspoon of the cinnamon.

3. **Prepare the filling.** Drain the juices from the can of peaches. In a medium bowl, toss the peaches and raspberries with the cornstarch, lemon juice, the remaining ½ cup of granulated sugar, and remaining 1 teaspoon of cinnamon. Gently toss together until the fruit is well coated.

4. **Fill and shape the dough.** Spoon the fruit mixture onto the center of the pie crust. Gently fold the pastry toward the center, bringing up about 1½ inches of the crust so it covers just the edge of the fruit mixture, folding and overlapping the edge to create pleats. Cut the cold butter into small cubes. Spread the butter cubes evenly across the top of the exposed fruit filling.

Continued on next page

5. **Glaze the dough.** In another small bowl, lightly beat the egg with a fork to create an egg wash. Use the pastry brush to glaze the top of the dough edges with the egg wash. Sprinkle the cinnamon sugar evenly over the galette.

6. **Bake the galette.** Place the baking sheet in the oven and bake for 20 to 25 minutes, or until the top of the dough turns lightly golden brown. Place the galette on a rack to cool for a few minutes before serving.

OOPS . . . Did the filling leak out through the crust while it was baking? It's normal for some particularly juicy fruits to leak. To avoid too much juice from leaking out, make sure you don't pile the fruit too high. You can also dust the pie crust lightly with all-purpose flour on both sides before filling and baking.

TRY THIS! Make a savory galette by using different ingredients for the filling, such as thinly sliced tomatoes and/or zucchini, tossed with salt, olive oil, and ground black pepper.

Farm-Fresh Strawberry Pie

Serves 8

Prep time: 20 minutes, plus 1 hour to chill / Cook time: 20 minutes

NO NUTS NO SOY VEGETARIAN

Sweet summer strawberries shine in this easy-to-make pie. If strawberries aren't in season, grab a bag of frozen strawberries and thaw them. Top the pie with whipped cream for an extra-special touch!

TOOLS AND EQUIPMENT

9-inch pie pan

Aluminum foil

Cutting board

Knife

Large microwave-safe bowl

Spoon

....

INGREDIENTS

Butter, for greasing

1 refrigerated pie crust, at room temperature

4 cups (2 pounds) fresh strawberries

1 cup granulated sugar

2 tablespoons cornstarch

¾ cup water

1. Preheat the oven to 450°F. Grease the pie pan with some butter. Unroll the pie crust and press it into the prepared pie pan. Place 2 layers of aluminum foil over the top of the crust and gently press down so the foil snuggly covers the top and sides of the crust. Bake for 8 minutes, then remove the foil and bake for another 5 minutes.

2. Make the filling. While the crust is baking, remove the leaves (called hulls) from the strawberries and cut the strawberries into quarters on a cutting board. In a large microwave-safe bowl, use a spoon to mix the strawberries with the sugar, cornstarch, and water. Microwave for 3 minutes, stir, then microwave for 2 more minutes.

3. Assemble the pie. Remove the crust from the oven. Pour the strawberry filling into the crust. Let cool in the pan at room temperature for 10 minutes, then refrigerate the pie for at least 1 hour, until the filling is set.

TRY THIS! Add strawberry Jell-O to the filling mixture for an even thicker, more flavorful filling.

Salted Caramel Peach Hand Pies

Makes 6 hand pies

Prep time: 15 minutes / Cook time: 25 minutes

NO NUTS **NO SOY** VEGETARIAN

These peach hand pies are amazing on their own, but the salted-caramel drizzle makes them over-the-top delicious! This recipe makes extra caramel sauce, so you can serve the rest as a dipping sauce, keep it for another recipe, or pour it over some ice cream!

TOOLS AND EQUIPMENT

Baking sheet

Parchment paper

Cutting board

Knife

Large microwave-safe bowl

Spoon

Fork

Pastry brush

Whisk

....

INGREDIENTS

FOR THE PIES

1 (14.5-ounce) can sliced peaches

⅓ cup packed light brown sugar

1 teaspoon cornstarch

¼ teaspoon ground cinnamon

1 teaspoon fresh lemon juice

2 frozen puff pastry sheets, thawed (1-pound package)

FOR THE SALTED CARAMEL SAUCE

2 tablespoons unsalted butter

¼ cup heavy (whipping) cream

½ cup packed light brown sugar

¼ teaspoon table salt

½ teaspoon vanilla extract

1. **Preheat the oven to 400°F.** Line the baking sheet with parchment paper.

2. **Make the filling.** Drain the juices from the can of peaches, then slice the peaches into smaller pieces on a cutting board and put them into a large microwave-safe bowl. Mix in the brown sugar, cornstarch, cinnamon, and lemon juice. Microwave for 2 minutes, stir, then microwave for 2 more minutes.

3. **Cut the pastry.** Unfold the puff pastry onto the cutting board and evenly cut each sheet into 3 long rectangles; use the folds as a cutting guide. Spoon roughly 3 tablespoons of filling onto the middle of the bottom half of each rectangle. (You'll use the remaining filling in step 5.)

4. **Form the hand pies.** Gently fold the top of each rectangle over the bottom half and pinch the edges together. Using a fork, gently poke 3 sets of holes at the top of each pastry, about ½ inch apart. This lets the steam out while the pies bake so the pastry is crisper. Then gently press the tines of the fork into the pastry edges to create a striped border design around all 4 sides. This helps seal the hand pies. Place the hand pies on the prepared baking sheet.

5. **Add the finishing touch.** With a pastry brush, brush a small amount of the juices from the reserved filling over the tops of the pastries.

6. **Bake the hand pies.** Place the baking sheet in the oven and bake for 20 to 25 minutes, or until the tops and edges are golden brown. Allow the pastries to cool on the baking sheet at room temperature for 10 minutes.

7. **Make the salted caramel sauce.** Wash and dry the microwave-safe bowl. In the bowl, combine the butter, heavy cream, and brown sugar. Microwave for 1 minute, stir, then microwave for 30 more seconds. The caramel will naturally bubble during the heating process, but watch it carefully to make sure it doesn't bubble up over the bowl. Repeat this process 2 to 4 more times, until the caramel reaches a deep golden color and is slightly thicker. Carefully take it out of the microwave, then whisk in the salt and vanilla.

8. **Add the salted caramel sauce.** Dip a whisk into the caramel sauce and, moving your hand slowly back and forth, drizzle the sauce over the hand pies, allowing the sauce to drip from the whisk onto the pastry. Let the sauce set for 5 to 10 minutes, then serve.

TRY THIS! Switch out the peaches for other sliced or small fruits, like apples, blueberries, cherries, or blackberries.

Quick Microwave Apple Crisp

Serves 1

Prep time: 10 minutes / Cook time: 5 minutes

REALLY FAST NO NUTS **NO SOY** VEGETARIAN

When you're craving dessert but don't want to bake a whole pie or cake, this single-serving apple crisp really hits the spot! We love Granny Smith apples, but you can use any apple that holds its shape during baking, such as Jonagold or Braeburn.

TOOLS AND EQUIPMENT

Vegetable peeler

Apple corer

Cutting board

Knife

Medium microwave-safe bowl

Paper towel

Small mixing bowl

Tablespoon

INGREDIENTS

1 medium apple

1 tablespoon granulated sugar

1 teaspoon cornstarch

2 tablespoons old-fashioned rolled oats

2 tablespoons packed light brown sugar

1 tablespoon all-purpose flour

¼ teaspoon ground cinnamon

1 tablespoon unsalted butter

1. **Microwave the fruit mix.** Peel, core, and dice the apple. Put the apple pieces in a medium microwave-safe bowl with the granulated sugar and cornstarch and mix to coat. Then cover with a paper towel and microwave for 3 minutes, watching the mix carefully toward the end of the time so it doesn't bubble over.

2. **Mix the dry ingredients.** In a small bowl, combine the oats, brown sugar, flour, and cinnamon, stirring with a tablespoon. Cut the butter into small cubes. Use your hands to press the cubes into the oat mixture, tossing the ingredients together until the mixture is crumbly. Sprinkle the topping over the apple mixture in the bowl.

3. **Microwave for 1 minute.** Stir the fruit mixture at the bottom a bit, microwave for 1 more minute, then serve.

TRY THIS! Add a bit of crumbled cooked bacon to the topping just before you microwave it for the last time. The salty, savory bacon balances the sweet, tart apple flavors in such a yummy way.

Chocolate Chess Pie

Serves 8

Prep time: 10 minutes / Cook time: 45 minutes

REALLY FAST NO NUTS NO SOY VEGETARIAN

Chess pie is a one-bowl, basic Southern pie that consists mostly of flour, butter, sugar, and eggs. This updated chocolate version is rich, creamy, and anything but basic!

TOOLS AND EQUIPMENT

Medium microwave-safe mixing bowl

9-inch pie pan

Large mixing bowl

Whisk

INGREDIENTS

4 tablespoons (½ stick) unsalted butter, plus more for greasing

1 refrigerated pie crust, at room temperature

1 cup granulated sugar

5 tablespoons unsweetened cocoa powder

2 large eggs

⅔ cup sweetened condensed milk

1 teaspoon vanilla extract

1. **Melt the butter.** Put the butter in a medium microwave-safe bowl and melt for 45 seconds. Whisk to fully melt all the butter, then set on the counter to cool.

2. **Preheat the oven to 350°F.** Lightly grease the pie pan with a little butter, then press the pie dough into the pie pan.

3. **Mix the ingredients.** In a large bowl, whisk together the sugar and cocoa powder. Whisk in the eggs, one at a time. Then whisk in the melted and cooled butter, along with the condensed milk and vanilla.

4. **Bake the pie.** Pour the filling into the crust. Bake for 45 minutes, or until the center is firm. Allow the pie to cool in the pan for at least 10 minutes before slicing.

DON'T HAVE IT? If you don't have sweetened condensed milk, you can use the same amount of heavy (whipping) cream instead.

Mini Pecan Pies

Makes 18 mini pies

Prep time: 15 minutes / Cook time: 20 minutes

NO SOY VEGETARIAN

These crunchy, sweet, nutty two-bite treats are delicious little snacks, perfect for when you're craving the fall flavors of pecan pie. Serve them with whipped cream or a drizzle of chocolate sauce.

TOOLS AND EQUIPMENT

24-cup mini muffin pan

Cutting board

3-inch round cookie cutter or small glass jar

Rolling pin

Large mixing bowl

Whisk

Teaspoon

....

INGREDIENTS

Nonstick cooking spray

1 refrigerated pie crust, at room temperature

2 cups pecan halves

½ cup packed light brown sugar

⅓ cup light corn syrup

1 teaspoon vanilla extract

1 large egg

1 large egg white

¼ teaspoon table salt

1. **Preheat the oven to 350°F.** Spray the muffin pan with nonstick cooking spray.

2. **Prepare the crust.** Unroll the pie crust onto a cutting board. Use the cookie cutter to cut out circles. Roll the extra dough into a ball, then roll it flat again with a rolling pin and cut out more circles. Repeat until you've used all the dough. You'll have about 18 circles. Press the dough circles into the bottom and up the sides of the prepared muffin cups to create mini pie crusts.

3. **Make the filling.** Put the pecan halves on the cutting board. Use the rolling pin to crush them into smaller pieces. Then sprinkle up to 2 tablespoons of the pecan bits evenly into each cup. In a large bowl, whisk together the brown sugar, corn syrup, vanilla, egg, egg white, and salt. Spoon 2 teaspoons of filling into each cup.

4. **Bake the pies.** Place the muffin pan in the oven and bake for 18 to 20 minutes, or until the centers are firm. Let cool completely in the pan before removing the pies and serving.

Single-Serve Microwave Blueberry Cobbler

Serves 1

Prep time: 5 minutes / Cook time: 5 minutes

REALLY FAST NO NUTS NO SOY VEGETARIAN

This fruit cobbler has layers of flavor and can satisfy that sweet tooth in less than 10 minutes, thanks to the microwave. You can use fresh or frozen blueberries; the amount and directions remain the same.

TOOLS AND EQUIPMENT

Medium microwave-safe bowl or large mug

Small mixing bowl

Whisk

INGREDIENTS

1 cup fresh or frozen blueberries

1 tablespoon unsalted butter

1 tablespoon packed light brown sugar

1 teaspoon ground cinnamon, divided

2 tablespoons all-purpose flour

2 tablespoons milk

2 tablespoons granulated sugar, divided

½ teaspoon vanilla extract

½ teaspoon baking powder

¼ teaspoon table salt

1. **Mix the ingredients.** In a medium microwave-safe bowl or large mug, mix the blueberries, butter, brown sugar, and ½ teaspoon of cinnamon. Microwave for 1 minute. Stir and then set aside to cool slightly.

2. **Make the topping.** In a small bowl, whisk together the remaining ½ teaspoon of cinnamon, the flour, milk, 1 tablespoon of granulated sugar, the vanilla, baking powder, and salt. Evenly sprinkle the mixture on top of the blueberry mixture.

3. **Microwave the cobbler.** Place the bowl in the microwave and microwave for 1 minute. If the dough is not fully cooked, microwave for 30 seconds more. Remove from the microwave and immediately sprinkle the remaining 1 tablespoon of granulated sugar over the top of the cobbler.

DON'T HAVE IT? If you don't have baking powder, you can use ½ teaspoon baking soda plus a squeeze of lemon juice.

No-Bake Candy Bar Pie

Serves 8
Prep time: 15 minutes, plus 1 hour chilling time

NO SOY VEGETARIAN

This candy pie is the ultimate sweet treat! With two kinds of chocolate candies, peanut butter, cream cheese, and whipped topping, it's no wonder this pie is a favorite that doesn't last long in my house. This is a great pie to make ahead of time, because you can freeze it for up to one month.

TOOLS AND EQUIPMENT

Cutting board

Knife

2 small mixing bowls

9-inch round ceramic or glass pie plate

Medium microwave-safe bowl

Whisk

Resealable plastic bag

Rolling pin

Large mixing bowl

Fork

Offset spatula

INGREDIENTS

3 regular or 9 fun-size Snickers candy bars (about 1¼ cups chopped), divided

6 regular or 15 miniature Reese's Peanut Butter Cups (about 1¼ cups chopped), divided

8 tablespoons (1 stick) unsalted butter, plus more for greasing

10 whole graham crackers

½ cup packed light brown sugar

¼ teaspoon table salt

1 (8-ounce) package cream cheese, at room temperature (see page 9)

½ cup creamy peanut butter

1 cup powdered sugar

8 ounces frozen whipped topping, thawed and divided

1. **Chop the candy.** Separately chop the Snickers bars and Reese's Peanut Butter Cups on a cutting board, then place in separate small bowls.

2. **Prepare the crust.** Lightly grease the pie plate with a little butter. Put the stick of butter in a medium microwave-safe bowl and melt for 45 seconds. Whisk to fully melt all the butter, then set on the counter to cool. Put the graham crackers in a large plastic bag, seal, and use a rolling pin to crush the crackers into tiny crumbs. Pour the graham cracker crumbs into a large bowl, then whisk in the brown sugar and salt. Add the melted butter and stir with a fork until well incorporated. Then, press the mixture into the prepared pie plate. Refrigerate the crust while you make the filling. Wash and dry the large mixing bowl.

Continued on next page

3. **Make the filling.** In the large bowl, use the spatula to mix the cream cheese, peanut butter, and powdered sugar. Fold in all the whipped topping except 1 cup, then gently fold in 1 cup of chopped Snickers and ½ cup of chopped Reese's.

4. **Assemble the pie.** Spread the filling over the crust, top with the remaining 1 cup of whipped topping, and use the spatula to smooth it out. Then sprinkle the remaining ¼ cup of Snickers and ¼ cup of Reese's on top. Refrigerate for at least 1 hour.

TRY THIS! Other chocolate candy bars that would work well with this pie are Twix, Milky Way, 3 Musketeers, and Kit Kat. You can also add more crunch to each bite by using crunchy peanut butter instead of creamy. Short on time? Use a store-bought graham cracker crust.

Chapter 6
Savory Snacks and Treats

Pepperoni Pizza Cups

Makes 12 pizza cups
Prep time: 10 minutes / Cook time: 25 minutes
5 INGREDIENTS OR LESS REALLY FAST NO NUTS **NO SOY**

Heartier than pizza rolls and faster than making a whole pizza, these pizza cups are totally snackable and shareable. My family loves these! It's easy to customize the toppings to satisfy each person's taste.

TOOLS AND EQUIPMENT

12-cup muffin pan

Cutting board

Knife or pizza cutter

Tablespoon

....

INGREDIENTS

Nonstick cooking spray

1 (13.8-ounce) tube refrigerated pizza crust or homemade dough (see page 116)

¾ cup pizza sauce

¾ cup shredded mozzarella cheese

12 to 18 slices pepperoni

1. Preheat the oven to 400°F. Spray the muffin pan with nonstick cooking spray.

2. Unroll the pizza dough. Roll out the dough onto a cutting board and use a knife or pizza cutter to cut the dough into 12 squares. Place 1 square in each prepared muffin cup, then use your fingers to gently press the dough to fit into the bottom and up the sides.

3. Add the pizza filling. Spoon 1 heaping tablespoon of pizza sauce into each pizza cup. Sprinkle 1 heaping tablespoon of mozzarella on top of the sauce. Cut the pepperoni slices in half, then add 2 or 3 pieces to each cup.

4. Bake the pizza cups. Place the muffin pan in the oven and bake for 18 to 22 minutes, or until the top crust is golden brown and the filling is hot. Allow to cool slightly in the pan before tipping the cups out of the pan and serving.

TRY THIS! Make Tex-Mex pizza cups: use a Mexican-style cheese blend instead of mozzarella, leave out the pepperoni, and add chopped jalapeños, black olives, and minced fresh cilantro. Serve with sour cream and salsa.

Cheesy Pesto Breadsticks

Makes 18 breadsticks
Prep time: 10 minutes / Cook time: 20 minutes
5 INGREDIENTS OR LESS REALLY FAST **NO SOY** VEGETARIAN

This savory snack proves that puff pastry isn't just for desserts. Make restaurant-quality breadsticks in a snap with just four ingredients. Delicious on their own, they're even better when dipped in the marinara sauce from the Baked Mozzarella Sticks (page 114).

TOOLS AND EQUIPMENT

Baking sheet

Parchment paper

Cutting board

Tablespoon

Pizza cutter

Medium microwave-safe bowl

Pastry brush

INGREDIENTS

1 frozen puff pastry sheet, thawed (half a 1-pound package)

1 (8-ounce) jar basil pesto sauce

¼ cup grated Parmesan cheese

4 tablespoons (½ stick) unsalted butter

1. Preheat the oven to 400°F. Line the baking sheet with parchment paper.

2. Make the filling. Unfold the puff pastry sheet on a large cutting board (or parchment paper on a clean countertop). Evenly spoon a thin layer of the pesto on top. Sprinkle the Parmesan evenly over the pesto.

3. Form the breadsticks. Using a pizza cutter, cut the pastry sheet into 9 strips, each 1 inch wide. Fold a strip in half lengthwise, pressing down gently as you fold so that one side sticks to the other. (Some filling will spill out during this process; that's okay. You can always spoon more on top of the breadsticks before baking.) Use your fingers to twist the breadstick in a couple of places. Place the twisted stick on the prepared baking sheet, then repeat for the remaining sticks, placing them about 1 inch apart. Cut each stick in half so that you have a total of 18 sticks.

4. Place the butter in a microwave-safe bowl. Microwave for 45 seconds, then whisk to completely melt the butter. Using a pastry brush, brush the butter onto the tops of the breadsticks.

5. Bake the breadsticks. Place the baking sheet in the oven and bake for 15 to 17 minutes, until the pastry turns golden brown. Allow the breadsticks to cool slightly on the baking sheet before serving.

Brunch Totchos

Serves 10 to 12
Prep time: 10 minutes / Cook time: 30 minutes
REALLY FAST NO NUTS NO SOY

Totchos (aka Tater Tot nachos) are a popular brunch item where we live in the Pacific Northwest. They're so much fun to make (and even more fun to eat!), combining fave breakfast ingredients served nacho-style.

TOOLS AND EQUIPMENT

Baking sheet

Aluminum foil

Medium microwave-safe bowl

Fork

Paper towel

Medium microwave-safe plate

....

INGREDIENTS

Nonstick cooking spray

1 (32-ounce) package frozen Tater Tots

4 large eggs

1 tablespoon milk

7 slices bacon

2 cups shredded cheddar cheese

1 tablespoon minced fresh parsley

½ teaspoon table salt

¼ teaspoon ground black pepper

Optional toppings: sour cream, chopped tomatoes, chopped chives

1. **Preheat the oven to 425°F.** Line the baking sheet with aluminum foil and spray with nonstick cooking spray. Spread out the frozen Tater Tots on the prepared baking sheet in an even layer. Bake for 20 minutes.

2. **Scramble the eggs and cook the bacon.** Meanwhile, in a medium microwave-safe bowl, beat together the eggs and milk. Microwave for 1 minute. Fluff up with a fork and microwave again for 45 seconds. Use a fork to break the scrambled egg into smaller pieces. Place a paper towel on a medium microwave-safe plate, arrange the bacon slices on the towel, and microwave the bacon for 4 to 5 minutes, just until it reaches your preferred level of crispiness.

3. **Top the tater tots.** Remove the Tater Tots from the oven and keep the oven turned on. Sprinkle the eggs and bacon over the Tater Tots, then the cheese and parsley. Season with the salt and pepper, then place back in the oven to bake for 10 more minutes. Serve warm with your favorite toppings.

Buffalo Chicken Phyllo Bites

Makes 12 bites

Prep time: 10 minutes / Cook time: 10 minutes

REALLY FAST NO NUTS **NO SOY**

These cheesy buffalo chicken bites are a big hit when friends come over. We love serving them for Game Day, and they're fast enough to make for a quick snack any other time. This is a great recipe for when you have leftover rotisserie chicken from dinner the night before. You can make these bites as spicy or as mild as you want by adjusting how much buffalo sauce you add.

TOOLS AND EQUIPMENT

Baking sheet

Parchment paper

Cutting board

Knife

Large mixing bowl

2 forks

Teaspoon

....

INGREDIENTS

1 (12-count) package frozen phyllo cups, thawed

2 scallions (green parts only)

1 cup rotisserie chicken meat

½ cup (4 ounces) cream cheese, at room temperature (see page 9)

2 tablespoons buffalo sauce

1 (8-ounce) package ranch dressing mix

¼ cup shredded cheddar cheese

1. **Preheat the oven to 350°F.** Line the baking sheet with parchment paper. Place the phyllo cups on the prepared baking sheet, arranging them about 2 inches apart.

2. **Make the filling.** On a cutting board, slice the scallion greens diagonally into thin pieces. In a large bowl, use 2 forks to shred the chicken into small bits. Add the cream cheese, buffalo sauce, ranch dressing mix, scallion greens, and cheddar cheese. Mix all the ingredients well, until there are no longer any large chunks of cream cheese. Spoon some of the filling into each phyllo cup until you've used up all the filling.

3. **Bake the phyllo cups.** Place the baking sheet in the oven and bake for 8 to 10 minutes, until the cups are crisp and the fillings are hot. Allow the buffalo chicken bites to cool for 1 minute on the baking sheet before serving.

DON'T HAVE IT? If you don't have phyllo cups, you can use wonton wrappers instead. Place the wrappers into the cups of a 12-cup muffin pan instead of using a baking sheet. Then stuff the cups with the chicken filling and bake according to the recipe directions.

SWITCH IT UP! Use this same filling to make another fun-filled handheld treat: buffalo chicken empanadas! Follow the directions for making the Mushroom Empanadas (page 122), but use the buffalo chicken filling instead of the mushroom filling. Serve with a side of blue cheese dressing.

TRY THIS! Use most of the same ingredients plus a few extras to make chicken taco cups. Substitute sour cream for the cream cheese, salsa for the buffalo sauce, and taco seasoning for the ranch dressing. Use either Mexican-style shredded cheese or cheddar cheese. Bake for 6 to 8 minutes. Top with chopped black olives, jalapeños, more sour cream and salsa, and/or chopped fresh cilantro.

Soft Pretzel Bites

Makes 40 to 50 bites
Prep time: 20 minutes / Cook time: 15 minutes

5 INGREDIENTS OR LESS NO DAIRY **NO NUTS** **NO SOY** VEGETARIAN

These soft pretzel bites are delicious served with your favorite cheese dip. You'll be using the stovetop in addition to the oven for this recipe. Boiling the pretzel bites briefly gives them that classic and oh-so-satisfying chewy pretzel texture.

TOOLS AND EQUIPMENT

Baking sheet

Parchment paper

Large mixing bowl

Whisk

Silicone spatula

Cutting board

Pastry cutter or knife

Large stockpot

Large slotted spoon

Small mixing bowl

Pastry brush

Cooling rack

....

INGREDIENTS

FOR THE DOUGH

1½ cups warm water

1 packet active dry yeast or instant yeast (2¼ teaspoons)

1 tablespoon granulated sugar

1 teaspoon table salt

3¾ cups all-purpose flour, plus more as needed and for rolling out the dough

FOR THE STOCKPOT

8 cups water

½ cup baking soda

FOR THE TOPPING

1 large egg

1 teaspoon water

Sea salt, for sprinkling

1. Position an oven rack in the upper third of the oven and preheat the oven to 425°F. Line the baking sheet with parchment paper.

2. **Make the dough.** In a large bowl, whisk together the warm water and yeast. Then whisk in the sugar and salt. Gradually add the flour and use a spatula to mix all the ingredients into a dough. If the dough is still wet, add more flour, 1 tablespoon at a time, just until the dough no longer is sticky. Lightly sprinkle a bit of flour on a large cutting board or clean countertop. Knead the dough on the floured surface for about 2 minutes, until it is soft and smooth and easily forms a ball.

3. **Shape the pretzel bites.** Divide the dough into 3 equal pieces. Form each piece into a rope, then gently roll with your hands back and forth until each

rope is about 1 inch thick. Use a pastry cutter or knife to cut each rope into pretzel bite pieces that are about 2 inches wide. (You should get 40 to 50 pieces.)

4. **Boil the pretzel bites.** In a large stockpot, bring the water and baking soda to a boil over high heat. Working in small batches, place a few pretzel bites (4 to 8) on a large slotted spoon, then dip them slowly into the boiling water. Boil for 20 to 30 seconds; as soon as the pretzels float to the surface, lift them out of the water with the slotted spoon, allowing the excess water to drain back into the pot. Place the pretzels on the prepared baking sheet, leaving about 2 inches of space between them. Repeat this process with the remaining dough pieces.

5. **Make the egg wash.** Crack the egg into a small bowl, add the water, and whisk together lightly. Brush the egg wash over the top of each pretzel bite and sprinkle with some sea salt.

6. **Bake the pretzel bites.** Place the baking sheet in the oven and bake for 3 to 5 minutes, just until the tops turn golden brown. Allow the pretzel bites to cool on the baking sheet for 5 minutes, then transfer to a rack to cool completely.

Easy Homemade Bagels

Makes 8 bagels

Prep time: 10 minutes / Cook time: 25 minutes

5 INGREDIENTS OR LESS   REALLY FAST   NO NUTS   NO SOY   VEGETARIAN

Save money and skip the bakery; homemade bagels are easier to make than you might think. These bagels are fluffier than the traditional chewy bakery versions, but they are also much faster to make. Spread them with your favorite schmear (cream cheese), or create a fun brunch bagel bar for friends and family with a variety of toppings!

TOOLS AND EQUIPMENT

2 baking sheets

Parchment paper

Large mixing bowl

Whisk

Silicone spatula

Large cutting board

Small mixing bowl

Pastry brush

Knife

INGREDIENTS

Nonstick cooking spray

2 cups all-purpose flour, plus more for shaping the dough

4 teaspoons baking powder

¾ teaspoon table salt

2 cups sour cream

1 large egg

1 teaspoon water

1. **Preheat the oven to 375°F.** Line 2 baking sheets with parchment paper, then spray the parchment paper with nonstick cooking spray.

2. **Mix the ingredients.** In a large bowl, whisk together the flour, baking powder, and salt. Using a spatula, mix in the sour cream.

3. **Knead the dough.** Lightly sprinkle a bit of extra flour on a large cutting board or clean countertop. Turn the dough out onto the floured surface and knead the dough for about 2 minutes. The dough should no longer feel sticky.

4. **Shape the bagels.** Divide the dough into 8 equal pieces and use your hands to shape each piece into a ball. Using the palms of your hands, flatten each ball to form a disk about 2 inches thick. Use your thumbs to push through the center of each circle to create the classic hole in the center. Place 4 bagels on each of the prepared baking sheets.

5. **Make the egg wash.** Crack the egg into a small bowl, add the water, and whisk together lightly. Then use a pastry brush to brush the egg wash on the tops of the bagels.

6. **Bake the bagels.** Place the baking sheets in the oven and bake for 25 minutes, or until the tops are golden brown. Allow the bagels to cool on the baking sheets for 5 minutes, then slice in half and serve.

DON'T HAVE IT? If you don't have sour cream, you can use an equal amount of Greek yogurt.

OOPS . . . Is your dough still sticky even after a few minutes of kneading it? Add a little more flour, 1 tablespoon at a time, and knead until the dough is no longer sticky.

TRY THIS! Create a variety of bagels by adding your favorite mix-ins to the dough before kneading and baking. To make cinnamon raisin bagels, add 1 tablespoon of granulated sugar and ½ teaspoon of ground cinnamon to the dry ingredients, then stir in 1 cup of raisins to the dough before kneading. To make cheesy everything bagels, add 1 cup of shredded cheddar cheese and 1 tablespoon of everything seasoning to the dry ingredients, then follow the rest of the recipe instructions.

Grab-and-Go Breakfast Frittatas

Makes 24 mini frittatas

Prep time: 10 minutes / Cook time: 20 minutes

5 INGREDIENTS OR LESS   REALLY FAST   NO GLUTEN   NO NUTS   NO SOY

These are some of my favorite bites for a quick grab-and-go breakfast for the whole family, but they're also great to reheat in the microwave for a fast afternoon snack. We like to double the recipe and make two batches at a time. Then we freeze one batch for up to two months and refrigerate the rest to eat during the week.

TOOLS AND EQUIPMENT

24-cup mini muffin pan

Paper towel

Medium microwave-safe plate

Large mixing bowl

Whisk

....

INGREDIENTS

Nonstick cooking spray

6 slices bacon

4 large eggs

2 tablespoons milk

½ cup shredded cheddar cheese

1 teaspoon dried chives

½ teaspoon table salt

¼ teaspoon ground black pepper

1. Preheat the oven to 350°F. Spray the mini muffin pan with nonstick cooking spray.

2. Cook the bacon. Place a paper towel on a medium microwave-safe plate. Place the bacon slices on the towel and microwave for 5 to 6 minutes, or until the bacon is cooked to your preferred crispness. Let cool slightly.

3. Mix the ingredients. In a large bowl, whisk together the eggs, milk, cheddar cheese, chives, salt, and pepper. Carefully break the bacon into small crumbles, then add the crumbles to the bowl and whisk to combine.

4. Bake the frittatas. Pour or spoon the egg mixture into the prepared muffin cups, filling each about three-fourths full so the frittatas have room to puff up as they bake. Place the muffin pan in the oven and bake for 18 to 20 minutes, until the filling is firm. Let the frittatas cool in the pan for 5 minutes before popping them out of the cups to serve.

DON'T HAVE IT? If you don't have dried chives, you can use dried parsley, dried basil, or almost any other dried green herb. No mini muffin pan? No problem! You can make this recipe in a 12-cup muffin pan as well—you'll have fewer frittatas but they will be larger.

SWITCH IT UP! The ingredients for these mini frittatas can easily be made into a quiche. Thaw a frozen ready-made pie crust and place it in a pie pan. Make the frittata filling and whisk in 1 additional egg. Pour the filling into the crust and bake at 400°F for 25 to 30 minutes, or until the center is firm.

TRY THIS! Make these frittatas vegetarian by leaving out the bacon and using a combination of your favorite veggies. We've made this recipe with diced bell peppers, chopped broccoli, frozen spinach, and chopped mushrooms. Just make sure to dice or chop the ingredients into similar-size pieces—smaller than 1 inch each—so they cook up evenly when baked.

Baked Mozzarella Sticks with Marinara Sauce

Makes 24 sticks

Prep time: 10 minutes, plus 30 minutes to chill / Cook time: 10 minutes

NO NUTS **NO SOY** VEGETARIAN

These sticks make delicious dinner side dishes or yummy anytime snacks for dipping. You can freeze them for up to one month, then air-fry or microwave them directly from the freezer to reheat. Just be sure to let them cool down completely after baking before freezing them.

TOOLS AND EQUIPMENT

Baking sheet

Parchment paper

3 medium-size shallow bowls

Large microwave-safe bowl

Whisk

INGREDIENTS

FOR THE MOZZA-RELLA STICKS

¼ cup all-purpose flour

1 large egg

1 tablespoon water

FOR THE MARI-NARA SAUCE

1 (28-ounce) can crushed tomatoes

½ cup Italian-flavored bread crumbs

½ teaspoon garlic powder

12 mozzarella sticks

1 teaspoon dried Italian seasoning

1 teaspoon granulated sugar

½ teaspoon table salt

¼ ground black pepper

1. Line the baking sheet with parchment paper.

2. **Prepare the coating.** In a shallow bowl, place the flour. In a second shallow bowl, beat the egg and water together. In a third shallow bowl, mix the bread crumbs and garlic powder.

3. **Coat the mozzarella sticks.** Cut each mozzarella stick in half crosswise. Coat one piece first with the flour, then with the egg wash, then with the bread crumbs. Set it on the prepared baking sheet. Repeat with the remaining sticks, leaving about 1 inch of space between them on the baking sheet.

4. **Chill the mozzarella sticks.** Place the baking sheet in the freezer and chill for 30 minutes. This helps "set" the cheese so it doesn't ooze out before the breading is crisped.

5. **Meanwhile, make the marinara sauce.** In a large microwave-safe bowl, whisk together the tomatoes, Italian seasoning, sugar, salt, and pepper. Microwave for 5 minutes at a time, whisking between, until the sauce thickens, 15 to 20 minutes.

6. **Preheat the oven to 400°F.** Place the baking sheet in the oven and bake for 6 to 8 minutes, until golden.

7. **Dig in!** Serve the warm mozzarella sticks with the marinara sauce for dipping.

Barbecue Chicken Bacon Pizza

Makes 1 (12-inch) pizza (4 to 6 snack servings)
Prep time: 15 minutes / Cook time: 20 minutes
NO NUTS NO SOY

This recipe combines some of my family's favorite pizza toppings: barbecue sauce, chicken, and bacon. You can use shredded or diced rotisserie chicken from the grocery store or your own leftover roast chicken. Baking the dough ahead is an important step, as it ensures you won't end up with overcooked toppings and undercooked crust.

TOOLS AND EQUIPMENT

Parchment paper

12-inch pizza pan

Pencil

Scissors

Large mixing bowl

Silicone spatula

Rolling pin

Pastry brush

Tablespoon

Cutting board

Knife

....

INGREDIENTS

FOR THE PIZZA DOUGH

1½ cups self-rising flour

1 cup plain Greek yogurt

2 tablespoons extra-virgin olive oil

FOR THE TOPPINGS

1 cup barbecue sauce

2 cups shredded mozzarella

cheese or pizza cheese blend

1½ cups rotisserie chicken meat

3 slices precooked bacon

1. **Preheat the oven to 450°F.** Place a sheet of parchment paper on the counter, invert the pizza pan over it, and trace a circle with a pencil. Cut out the circle with a scissors and fit the paper into the pizza pan.

2. **Make the pizza dough.** In a large bowl, use a spatula to mix the flour and yogurt. Use your hands to shape the dough into a ball. Place the dough in the prepared pizza pan and use a rolling pin to roll it out until it's flat, fits to the pan edge, and is about ¼ inch thick. Use a pastry brush to brush the olive oil over the top of the dough.

3. **Bake the crust.** Place the pizza pan in the oven and bake the crust for 5 minutes. Remove the pizza pan from the oven and turn the oven temperature up to 500°F.

4. **Add the sauce and cheese.** Spoon the barbecue sauce into the center of the crust and spread it evenly, leaving about a 1-inch border around the edge. Sprinkle the cheese evenly over the pizza.

5. **Add the chicken and bacon.** Cut the chicken and bacon into bite-size pieces. Scatter them on top of the cheese.

6. **Bake the pizza.** Return the pizza pan to the oven and bake for 12 to 14 minutes, or until the edges of the crust are crisp and browned, and the cheese is bubbly and melted.

DON'T HAVE IT? If you don't have self-rising flour, you can make your own by sifting together 1½ teaspoons baking powder and 1½ cups all-purpose flour.

OOPS . . . While mixing the dough, is it still too sticky? Add more flour, 1 tablespoon at a time, until the dough is no longer sticky. If the dough is too dry, try adding 1 tablespoon of yogurt or water a little at a time.

TRY THIS! This recipe has so many variation options. Ranch dressing would be a delicious substitute for barbecue sauce, or use salami instead of bacon.

Ham and Cheese Drop Biscuits

Makes 10 biscuits

Prep time: 10 minutes / Cook time: 25 minutes

REALLY FAST NO NUTS **NO SOY**

Drop biscuits are some of the easiest biscuits to make . . . and the tastiest! All the ingredients are combined in one bowl, and they bake up to create the cheesiest, fluffiest, butteriest biscuits. Any biscuits that aren't gobbled up right away can be frozen for up to two months and reheated.

TOOLS AND EQUIPMENT

2 baking sheets

Parchment paper

Large mixing bowl

Whisk

Cutting board

Knife

Wooden spoon

Large cookie scoop

....

INGREDIENTS

2 cups all-purpose flour

1 tablespoon baking powder

½ teaspoon garlic powder

1 teaspoon table salt

¼ teaspoon ground black pepper

8 tablespoons (1 stick) unsalted butter, cold

1 cup diced ham

1 cup shredded cheddar cheese

1 cup buttermilk

1. Preheat the oven to 450°F. Line 2 baking sheets with parchment paper.

2. Mix the dry ingredients. In a large bowl, whisk together the flour, baking powder, garlic powder, salt, and pepper.

3. Cube the butter. Use a knife to cut the butter into small cubes. Then with your hands, press the butter cubes into the flour mixture and mix all the ingredients well. The mixture will be crumbly, and it's okay if there are a few small pieces of butter in the mix; just make sure there aren't large chunks that haven't been pressed into the flour mixture.

4. Mix in the final ingredients. With a wooden spoon, stir in the ham and cheese. Slowly pour in the buttermilk, stirring until combined. The dough will be lumpy.

5. **Form and bake the biscuits.** Using a large cookie scoop or ¼-cup measuring cup, scoop up large mounds of the dough and place them on the prepared baking sheets about 2 inches apart. Place the baking sheets in the oven and bake for 18 to 22 minutes, or until the biscuits are golden brown and puffed up.

DON'T HAVE IT? If you don't have garlic powder, you can simply leave it out. Garlic powder gives the biscuits a salty seasoning that many people are familiar with (think Red Lobster cheddar biscuits), but these biscuits are just as tasty without the garlic powder.

OOPS . . . While mixing the dough, does it feel too dry? You can add more buttermilk, 1 tablespoon at a time, and stir until it's well combined.

TRY THIS! Substitute bits of cooked bacon for the ham to make bacon and cheese biscuits. These are also delicious when you add some fresh or dried chopped parsley to the flour mixture.

Garlic Herb Flatbread

Serves 6 to 8

Prep time: 10 minutes / Cook time: 20 minutes

5 INGREDIENTS OR LESS REALLY FAST NO NUTS **NO SOY** VEGETARIAN

Tasty garlic bread couldn't be simpler! Enjoy this flatbread as a snack on its own, as a side dish to soak up any remaining spaghetti sauce on your plate, or as a topping with your favorite vegetables.

TOOLS AND EQUIPMENT

Baking sheet

Parchment paper

Medium microwave-safe bowl

Whisk

Pastry brush

Cutting board

Knife

....

INGREDIENTS

4 tablespoons (½ stick) unsalted butter

2 tablespoons dried parsley

½ teaspoon garlic powder

1 (13.8-ounce) tube refrigerated pizza dough or homemade pizza dough (see page 116)

½ teaspoon sea salt

¼ teaspoon ground black pepper

1. **Preheat the oven to 350°F.** Line the baking sheet with parchment paper.

2. **Mix the topping ingredients.** In a medium microwave-safe bowl, microwave the butter for 45 seconds, until partially melted. Whisk in the parsley and garlic powder.

3. **Prepare the dough.** Unroll the pizza dough and fit it onto the prepared baking sheet. Use a pastry brush to brush the herbed butter evenly on the dough. Sprinkle the dough with the salt and pepper.

4. **Bake the flatbread.** Place the baking sheet in the oven and bake for 20 minutes, or until the edges are golden brown. Let cool on the baking sheet for about 5 minutes, then slice and serve.

TRY THIS! Top the baked flatbread with spoonfuls of homemade or store-bought bruschetta toppings, or add chopped mushrooms to the crust before baking.

Tex-Mex Vegetarian Nachos

Serves 8 to 10

Prep time: 15 minutes / Cook time: 15 minutes

NO NUTS **NO SOY** VEGETARIAN

Perfect for parties or post-game gatherings and study groups, this healthy snack is super-satisfying and totally tasty. It's colorful, crunchy, and packed with flavor. Pile on the toppings or put them in individual bowls to create a nacho bar and let each person top their own!

TOOLS AND EQUIPMENT

Baking sheet

Parchment paper

Colander

Medium mixing bowl

Tablespoon

Cutting board

Knife

....

INGREDIENTS

1 (15-ounce) bag tortilla chips

1 (15-ounce) can pinto beans

1 tablespoon taco seasoning

1 sprig fresh cilantro

1 (8-ounce) package shredded Mexican cheese blend

1 (8-ounce) container pico de gallo

Optional toppings: sliced jalapeños, black olives, sour cream, avocado slices or guacamole

Lime wedges, for serving

1. Preheat the oven to 400°F. Line the baking sheet with parchment paper. Spread out the tortilla chips on the baking sheet, with some chips overlapping as necessary. Bake for 5 minutes. The tops of the chips will turn slightly darker. Remove from the oven and keep the oven on.

2. Prepare the toppings. Drain and rinse the pinto beans in the colander. Put the pinto beans in a medium bowl. Sprinkle the taco seasoning over the beans and mix with a spoon. On a cutting board, chop 1 tablespoon of the cilantro leaves.

3. Bake the nachos. Spoon the beans over the chips. Sprinkle the cheese evenly across the top, then bake for 8 to 12 minutes, just until the cheese starts bubbling and melts.

4. Add the toppings. Top the nachos with the pico de gallo and the cilantro. Then serve with your choice of toppings and with lime wedges on the side.

Mushroom Empanadas

Makes 8 to 10 empanadas

Prep time: 10 minutes / Cook time: 20 minutes

REALLY FAST NO DAIRY NO NUTS **NO SOY** VEGETARIAN

Empanadas are yummy baked or fried savory stuffed pastries. You can find different versions of these baked pastries in many different cultures. These empanadas are made easier and faster, thanks to the packaged crescent dough sheets.

TOOLS AND EQUIPMENT

Baking sheet

Parchment paper

Large round cookie cutter, 3½ to 4 inches in diameter

Rolling pin

Cutting board

Knife

Medium microwave-safe bowl

Tablespoon

2 small mixing bowls

Fork

Pastry brush

INGREDIENTS

1 (8-ounce) tube refrigerated or frozen crescent dough sheet, thawed if frozen

1 cup fresh baby bella or cremini mushrooms

1 garlic clove

1 tablespoon olive oil

1 teaspoon fresh or dried thyme

½ teaspoon table salt

¼ teaspoon black pepper

1 large egg, separated

1. **Preheat the oven to 400°F.** Line the baking sheet with parchment paper.

2. **Prepare the dough.** Unroll the sheet of crescent dough onto the prepared baking sheet. Using a large round cookie cutter, cut out 8 circles. Gather any extra dough into a ball, roll flat using a rolling pin, and cut out another 1 or 2 circles. Discard any leftover dough. Place the circles about 1 inch apart on the prepared baking sheet.

3. **Make the filling.** Finely dice the mushrooms, then peel and mince the garlic clove. Put the mushrooms, garlic, and olive oil in a medium microwave-safe bowl and microwave for 1 minute. Add the thyme, salt, and pepper to the bowl and stir to combine. Spoon about ½ tablespoonful of filling on the center of each dough circle.

4. **Shape the empanadas.** Place the egg white in a small bowl, then put the egg yolk in another small bowl. Use a fork to lightly beat the egg white, then to lightly beat the egg yolk. With a pastry brush or your fingers, brush

some of the egg white onto the outside edge of one half of each dough circle. Fold one side of the dough over to meet the other side, so that it forms a half-circle. Use the fork to press down and seal the edges, creating a nice pattern around the curved part of the half-circles. Dip the pastry brush into the beaten yolk and lightly brush the top of each empanada. This is what gives them their classic golden-brown top when they bake.

5. **Bake the empanadas.** Place the baking sheet in the oven and bake for 15 to 17 minutes, or until the tops are shiny and golden brown.

DON'T HAVE IT? If you can't find a package of crescent roll sheets, you can also use store-bought refrigerated pie crust.

TRY THIS! For a meaty version, replace the mushroom filling in this recipe with the filling from Buffalo Chicken Phyllo Bites (page 106).

Homemade Sesame Crackers
and Easy Cheesy Dip

Makes 6 to 7 dozen crackers

Prep time: 20 minutes / Cook time: 20 minutes

NO NUTS NO SOY VEGETARIAN

Impress your friends and family by making your own crackers and dip from scratch! They look fancy enough for any charcuterie board, but your friends don't need to know just how easy these actually are to make! Be sure to roll the dough super thin for crispier crackers; for chewier crackers, leave them a little thicker.

TOOLS AND EQUIPMENT

2 baking sheets

Parchment paper

Large mixing bowl

Whisk

Silicone spatula

Rolling pin

2 small mixing bowls

Pastry brush

Pizza cutter or knife

Cooling rack

INGREDIENTS

FOR THE CRACKERS

2 cups all-purpose flour

¼ cup shredded Parmesan cheese

3 tablespoons white sesame seeds

2 tablespoons poppy seeds

1 teaspoon baking powder

½ teaspoon table salt

⅓ cup warm water, plus more as needed

⅓ cup vegetable oil

FOR THE TOPPINGS

1 large egg white

¼ cup grated Parmesan cheese

1 tablespoon white sesame seeds

1 tablespoon poppy seeds

FOR THE CHEESE DIP

1 (8-ounce) package cream cheese, at room temperature (see page 9)

1 cup sour cream

1 (1-ounce) package ranch dressing mix or ½ teaspoon garlic powder

2 cups shredded cheddar cheese

Continued on next page

1. Preheat the oven to 400°F. Line 2 baking sheets with parchment paper.

2. **Mix the ingredients.** In a large bowl, whisk together the flour, Parmesan cheese, sesame seeds, poppy seeds, baking powder, and salt. Slowly add the warm water and stir with a spatula. Then add the oil and stir everything together until the dough starts to form a smooth ball; add more water by the teaspoonful, as needed.

3. **Shape the crackers.** Divide the dough into 2 balls. Using a rolling pin, flatten each ball of dough into a rectangle, about 9 by 13 inches.

4. **Top the crackers.** In a small bowl, whisk the egg white, then use a pastry brush to brush it over the dough. In another small bowl, whisk together the Parmesan, sesame seeds, and poppy seeds for the topping. Sprinkle the topping evenly over both dough rectangles.

5. **Score the dough.** Using a pizza cutter or knife, "score" the dough to create the cracker shapes. To do this, gently cut 7 to 8 score lines about 1 inch wide into the top of each rectangle, being careful not to cut through to the bottom. Then make about 11 to 12 score lines the opposite way, also about 1 inch apart. You should have 70 to 80 crackers scored, depending on how thin or thick you rolled your dough, and the size of each cracker.

6. **Bake the crackers.** Place the baking sheets in the oven and bake for 15 to 18 minutes, or until the crackers are golden brown. Remove from the oven and immediately snap the crackers apart along the scored lines. (If left too long, they sometimes puff a bit and won't snap along the lines as well.) Place the crackers on a rack to cool for 10 minutes.

7. **Make the dip.** Wash and dry the large bowl. In the bowl, mix all the ingredients for the dip. Serve with the crackers.

TRY THIS! Everyone loves a fruit and cheese board. Place these crackers and the dip on a cutting board, then surround with salami slices, olives, almonds, grapes, strawberries, blueberries, and raspberries. Such fun to enjoy with friends!

Pull-Apart Cheesy Bread

Serves 8

Prep time: 10 minutes / Cook time: 30 minutes

REALLY FAST NO NUTS NO SOY VEGETARIAN

Looking for an easy recipe that'll give you that cheese pull everyone loves to see in slo-mo? This recipe is it! This is the ultimate pull-apart bread, with loads of cheese, big garlic flavor, and silky butter in every bite.

TOOLS AND EQUIPMENT

Baking sheet

Parchment paper

Cutting board

Bread knife

Medium microwave-safe bowl

Whisk

Aluminum foil

....

INGREDIENTS

1 (16-ounce) loaf French bread

8 tablespoons (1 stick) unsalted butter

1 teaspoon garlic powder

½ teaspoon onion powder

1 cup shredded cheddar cheese

1 cup shredded mozzarella cheese

2 teaspoons dried parsley

1. **Preheat the oven to 375°F.** Line the baking sheet with parchment paper.

2. **Slice the bread.** Using a bread knife, make slices into the loaf about 1 inch apart, cutting halfway through (don't cut all the way to the bottom) in one direction. Then repeat to make slices in the opposite direction so you create a crisscross pattern of slices. Place the bread on the prepared baking sheet.

3. **Make the filling.** Put the butter, garlic powder, and onion powder in a medium microwave-safe bowl and microwave for 30 seconds, then whisk until completely melted. Pour the butter mixture evenly over the open cuts in the bread. Sprinkle both cheeses into the cracks, gently pushing the cheese down into the slices, and sprinkle the parsley on top.

4. **Bake the bread.** Cover the bread loosely with aluminum foil and bake for 20 minutes. Remove the foil and bake uncovered for 10 more minutes, until the cheese has fully melted and the top of the bread is golden brown. Allow to cool on the baking sheet for 5 minutes.

Baking Terms You Should Know
A Glossary of Common Terms

You may notice certain terms are used frequently in these recipes. Here's a brief explanation of some of the most common baking terms.

At room temperature: the temperature of an ingredient after it has been brought out of the refrigerator or freezer and left to sit on the counter until no longer cold or stiff; it's about the same temperature as the room.

Beat: to mix vigorously with a fork or hand mixer until the ingredients are well combined.

Combine: to mix two or more ingredients.

Cream: to mix ingredients using a hand mixer or fork until the ingredients are well combined, smooth, and creamy.

Divided: when the listed quantity of an ingredient is split and used separately in a recipe.

Drizzle: to drip icing or glaze over baked goods using the edge of a spoon, fork, or whisk.

Dust: to very lightly sprinkle flour, cocoa powder, or sugar over baked goods.

Fold: to gently bring together ingredients by using a spatula to place one over another, until fully combined.

Ganache: a smooth, shiny mixture of melted chocolate and cream.

Glaze: a sugary, liquid topping for baked goods that's usually thinner than frosting or icing.

Grate: to shred with a handheld grater.

Grease: to use butter or oil to coat the inside of a baking pan or a baking sheet.

Knead: to use your hands to gently press into a dough and turn it, forming a smooth, elastic ball.

Line: to cover bakeware with parchment paper or aluminum foil so that the baked goods don't stick to the pan.

Mince: to use a knife to finely cut food into tiny pieces.

Set: when baked goods are evenly cooked and no longer loose in the center.

Softened: an ingredient such as cream cheese or butter that is soft enough to easily mix in with other ingredients but is not melted; also referred to as "at room temperature."

Stir: to mix ingredients in a circular motion using a spoon, spatula, or whisk.

Toss: to combine ingredients, usually by hand or with spoons, by lifting the ingredients in the bottom of a bowl and bringing them to the top.

Whisk: to use a whisk to combine ingredients evenly in a circular motion.

Zest: to use a hand zester or grater to remove small pieces of the outer peel of lemons, limes, or oranges to extract more flavor; the resulting tiny pieces of peel are also called the zest.

MEASUREMENT CONVERSIONS

Volume Equivalents	U.S. Standard	U.S. Standard (ounces)	Metric (approximate)
Liquid	2 tablespoons	1 fl. oz.	30 mL
	¼ cup	2 fl. oz.	60 mL
	½ cup	4 fl. oz.	120 mL
	1 cup	8 fl. oz.	240 mL
	1½ cups	12 fl. oz.	355 mL
	2 cups or 1 pint	16 fl. oz.	475 mL
	4 cups or 1 quart	32 fl. oz.	1 L
	1 gallon	128 fl. oz.	4 L
Dry	⅛ teaspoon	—	0.5 mL
	¼ teaspoon	—	1 mL
	½ teaspoon	—	2 mL
	¾ teaspoon	—	4 mL
	1 teaspoon	—	5 mL
	1 tablespoon	—	15 mL
	¼ cup	—	59 mL
	⅓ cup	—	79 mL
	½ cup	—	118 mL
	⅔ cup	—	156 mL
	¾ cup	—	177 mL
	1 cup	—	235 mL
	2 cups or 1 pint	—	475 mL
	3 cups	—	700 mL
	4 cups or 1 quart	—	1 L
	½ gallon	—	2 L
	1 gallon	—	4 L

Oven Temperatures

Fahrenheit	Celsius (approximate)
250°F	120°C
300°F	150°C
325°F	165°C
350°F	180°C
375°F	190°C
400°F	200°C
425°F	220°C
450°F	230°C

Weight Equivalents

U.S. Standard	Metric (approximate)
½ ounce	15 g
1 ounce	30 g
2 ounces	60 g
4 ounces	115 g
8 ounces	225 g
12 ounces	340 g
16 ounces or 1 pound	455 g

Index

W

Whisk, defined, 130
White chocolate
  Sugar Cookie Confetti Cake, 79–80
  Zesty Coconut Lime
    Macaroons, 46–47

Y

Yeast, 8

Z

Zest, defined, 130
Zesty Coconut Lime Macaroons, 46–47

Acknowledgments

Many thanks to my in-house team of teenage taste testers, Ethan and Cate, who helped me perfect the recipes in this cookbook. I always love cooking and baking with you two!

Thanks also to teen recipe testers Carter, Evan, Kaden, and Lauren. You are fantastic bakers!

The cookbook couldn't have come to life without the amazing, supportive Rockridge Press team. Special thanks to my super-awesome editor, Laura Apperson.

Last but not least, huge thanks to friends, family, and blog readers. Thank you for always inspiring me to keep cooking and baking.

About the Author

 This is Marlynn Jayme Schotland's second cookbook. She is also the author of the *Ninja Foodi Pressure Cooker Meal Prep Cookbook*. Her recipes have been featured on *The Drew Barrymore Show*, as well as in *O* magazine, *Good Housekeeping*, *Shape* magazine, and more. She is a longtime food, wine, and travel blogger and shares her original recipes, wine pairings and wine notes, and travel guides on her site UrbanBlissLife.com. You can connect with her on all social media platforms: @UrbanBlissLife. Marlynn lives in Portland, Oregon, on the edge of beautiful wine country with her husband, their two teenagers, and a quirky black lab retriever.

Printed in the USA
CPSIA information can be obtained
at www.ICGtesting.com
CBHW041924230524
8965CB00009B/3